THE MEGALITHIC MONUMENTS
OF BRITAIN & IRELAND

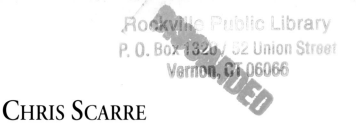
CHRIS SCARRE

THE MEGALITHIC MONUMENTS
OF BRITAIN & IRELAND

with 175 illustrations, 20 in color

Thames & Hudson

Frontispiece *The stone circle at Castlerigg, Cumbria.*

This edition first published in 2007 in paperback in the United States of America by Thames & Hudson Inc., 500 Fifth Avenue, New York, New York 10110

thamesandhudsonusa.com

Library of Congress Catalog Card Number 2006908249

ISBN-13: 978-0-500-28666-1
ISBN-10: 0-500-28666-3

Printed and bound in Singapore by Star Standard Industries (Pte Ltd)

CONTENTS

CHAPTER ONE

Monuments, society & landscape

Twas in that deluge of Historie, that memorie of these British Monuments utterly perished: the Discovery whereof I doe here endeavour (for want of written Record) to work-out and restore ... by comparing those I have seen with one another ... to make the Stones give Evidence for themselves.
John Aubrey, *Monumenta Britannica*, 1693, 32

THE MEGALITHIC MONUMENTS OF BRITAIN AND IRELAND HAVE BEEN the subject of scholarly investigation since at least the 17th century. In the same decade that John Aubrey was completing his *Monumenta Britannica*, with its descriptions and diagrams of Avebury and Stonehenge, Welsh antiquarian Edward Lhywd was recounting the discovery of the passage tomb at Newgrange in Ireland. The number and sheer diversity of these megalithic monuments was soon appreciated, with stone rows and circles alongside chambered tombs of various kinds. Henges and cursus monuments that lacked stone elements were early recognized as belonging to the same general category of prehistoric monuments. The first serious investigations had to wait until the 19th century, when excavations (some extremely cursory) were conducted at a large proportion of the visible sites. It was only towards the end of the 19th century, notably in General Pitt-Rivers' fieldwork on Cranborne Chase, that higher standards of excavation, observation and recording began to prevail, and that the true nature of the many monuments involving turf and timber structures came to be discovered.

Prehistoric monuments have remained a focus of research for British and Irish archaeologists throughout the 20th century. The megalithic tombs and circles that attracted the attention of the

Two travellers take shelter beneath the capstone of the megalithic tomb of Pentre Ifan in southwest Wales, from Archaeologia Cambrensis, *1865.*

6

early antiquaries now take their proper place as but one of the many types of monument that characterized the transformation of the landscape during the Neolithic – from the arrival of pottery and domesticates some 6000 years ago to the beginning of the Bronze Age around 1700 years later. The conclusion must be that these monuments represented for Neolithic communities a particular way of responding to changing social and symbolic needs and to new ritual practices: ways of processing the dead, of gathering for ceremonies, of marking out and embellishing locations that were of special and perhaps sacred significance.

In this short book the aim is to provide an introduction to the wide range of British and Irish Neolithic monuments. In such a broad subject, diversity is one of the key features, and this includes the materials that were used to construct the monuments, which might be of timber or stone, but also often involved the digging of ditches and the building of enclosures, mounds and cairns. Among the stone-built monuments, those of megalithic construction (built of 'megalithic' or extravagantly large slabs) have a prominent and distinguished place.

Brownshill, Co. Clare, Ireland: weighing 100 tonnes, the capstone of this megalithic tomb is one of the largest in Europe.

Many of the major monuments were of dry-stone construction, however, and some of the most impressive feats of Neolithic engineering, such as the corbelled vault of Newgrange, employ stones of relatively modest proportions. For much of lowland Britain, furthermore, the emphasis is on monuments of earth and timber, though 'earth' in this context is taken to include turf or chalk. The term 'cairn', by contrast, is reserved for mounds of rubble construction that are generally restricted to the highland areas where stone is the obvious and most readily available building material.

In terms of timescale, the story opens with the beginning of the Neolithic, and continues down to the Early Bronze Age. It is clear, however, that many monuments of megalithic construction – such as the stone rows of Dartmoor or the boulder burials of southwest Ireland – were built in later periods. Burial mounds, too, are a feature that continues into the Bronze Age and beyond, and Bronze Age round mounds sometimes occur in clusters close to major Neolithic monuments. Thus the division between Neolithic and Bronze Age that is followed here is somewhat arbitrary, and monument traditions develop seamlessly from one period into the next. Many of the classic monument forms, such as henges, cursus monuments, long mounds and passage graves, are, however, restricted to the Neolithic period and were no longer built after 2300 BC.

Mesolithic Britain and the Continent

Some 6000 years ago the people of Britain and Ireland abandoned their dependence on hunting and gathering and began to cultivate cereals and raise herds of cattle, sheep and pigs. There has been considerable debate as to how farming was introduced to these islands. It is clear that the cereals and the animal species involved, were brought from neighbouring regions of the Continent, where farming had already been practised for several centuries. The same is true of pottery, which had not been made in Britain by hunter-gatherer communities, perhaps because it was too heavy and fragile for these relatively mobile groups to carry round with them, or perhaps simply because they had no need for pottery vessels. Thus, when pottery and domesticates first appeared in Britain in around 4000 BC, they did so via contacts with Continental Europe.

To place this in a broader context, we must go back to the period immediately following the end of the last Ice Age, around 9600 BC, when the ice sheets that had covered Scotland had melted, but sea-level was still much lower than it is today. For several thousand years the area now occupied by the North Sea was a vast marshy lowland, punctuated near its centre by a group of hills that survive today as the submarine feature known as the Dogger Bank. The marshy North Sea

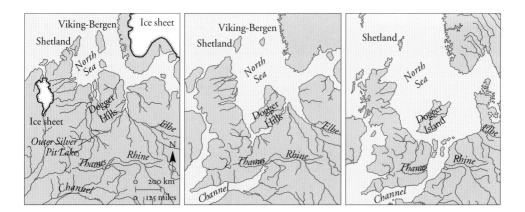

lowland was an environment rich in plants and animal resources, notably fish and waterfowl, with forest animals in its drier parts. A scatter of hunter-gatherer communities occupied this terrain, extending from eastern Britain to the Netherlands and Denmark. Material evidence of their presence survives in the form of flint and antler implements that are occasionally brought up in fishing nets from the bed of the North Sea. At the southern edge of this wetland, the Thames, the Rhine and the Seine flowed together into a single estuary which ran westwards along what later became the English Channel to join the Atlantic.

As sea-level rose, this marshy lowland was steadily flooded, and Britain was eventually cut off from the rest of Europe in around 6500 BC. For a while, the Dogger Bank survived as a small island, before it too was swallowed up beneath the waves. The changing geography is reflected in the flintwork. Before 6500 BC, the flint tool traditions of Britain and the neighbouring part of the Continent were relatively similar, and had developed in step with each other. After 6500 BC, however, the two traditions diverge, and British Mesolithic flintwork becomes increasingly insular. Yet it is unlikely that contact was entirely broken, not least since the use of boats at this period is well established: there is Mesolithic material from most Scottish islands, for example, and Mesolithic shell middens are found on Oronsay, which is too small an island to have supported a permanent hunter-gatherer population. Furthermore, specific island raw materials such as Rhum bloodstone and Arran pitchstone were exploited and traded both to the mainland of western Scotland and to northern Ireland. Wider expanses of sea may have proved more of a challenge to Mesolithic sailors, but there is ample evidence for even longer sea crossings at much earlier dates in other parts of the world. There are therefore no grounds to suggest that Britain need necessarily have been cut off from contacts with the Continent when the North Sea basin was flooded.

The progressive separation of Britain and Ireland from the continent of Europe resulting from Holocene sea-level rise: (left) around 11,000 BC; (centre) around 8000 BC; (right) around 5000 BC.

9

It must certainly have been by sea that the first domesticates reached Britain in around 4000 BC. There is tantalizing evidence from Ferriter's Cove in southern Ireland for the arrival of domesticates even earlier, in the form of cattle remains dated to 4495–4165 BC. Whether this can be held to imply direct contact between Mesolithic communities of this region and early farming communities of Continental Europe (possibly northwest France), however, remains open to question. Domestic plants and animals are more likely to have crossed the relatively narrow seas between southeast England and the Low Countries or northern France than the much wider and rougher stretch of sea between southern Ireland and Brittany. Detailed analysis of early domestic cattle bones has shown a close correspondence in size between those of southern Britain and the Paris basin, indicating that northern France may be the place where the first British domesticates originated. At all events, the transport of cattle and pig to Britain would have required seaworthy boats of relatively substantial size.

The nature of the 'Neolithic transition'

It is possible that agriculture was introduced to Britain by farmers who arrived from the Continent and displaced the indigenous hunter-gatherer communities. An alternative view, however, holds that British hunter-gatherers themselves adopted the domesticates through contacts with their Continental neighbours. If we accept this, then the same people were now growing plants and raising animals who a few generations before – or indeed a few years earlier – had been hunting and gathering.

Archaeologists who would argue for continuity with Mesolithic lifestyles emphasize the likely mobility of early Neolithic communities in southern Britain. We know, for example, that these communities held domestic cattle in high regard, and we may envisage the regular movement of cattle herds between seasonal pastures. Several key elements of the classic agricultural lifestyle are scarce or absent from Britain, including (in most areas) Neolithic houses or the field systems that would be expected to characterize a stable arable land-use. Thus, the argument goes that while the Neolithic farmers in Britain may have incorporated domestic plants and animals along with other novel elements such as pottery and burial monuments, their lifestyle differed in fundamental ways from the pattern of settled farming familiar to us from later periods. The monuments, indeed, may have provided fixed points or markers in a landscape of relative fluidity and mobility.

There is, however, another side to this argument. It is clear that the cultivation of cereals was practised from the very beginning of the Neolithic period, and these imported domesticates would have needed careful tending to survive. Ethnography suggests that people would have had to remain close to their crops for at least the months between sowing and harvesting. Furthermore, while Neolithic houses are very scarce in southern Britain, they are much more numerous in Ireland. Neolithic field systems, too, have been found in certain areas, such as Céide fields in western Ireland, or Fengate in eastern England, though it is true that the extensive Late Bronze Age and Iron Age field systems of south-central and southwestern Britain do not seem to have had Neolithic antecedents. The conclusion may be that Neolithic lifestyles were very varied, and that we should be cautious about applying evidence from one area of Britain and Ireland to the whole archipelago.

Further insight into the Neolithic transition has been provided by recent studies of diet, based on the isotopic composition of human bones. Mesolithic and Neolithic human skeletons from coastal regions of South Wales and western Scotland have shown evidence of a high consumption of marine foods during the Mesolithic. This is a pattern that would be expected given the coastal location of many of the sites from which these remains derive. Indeed, those very same sites often contain middens of marine shells. At the beginning of the Neolithic, however, this pattern changes abruptly, and the dietary emphasis switches to exclusively terrestrial resources. This dramatic shift may be in part a cultural phenomenon, related to a deliberate

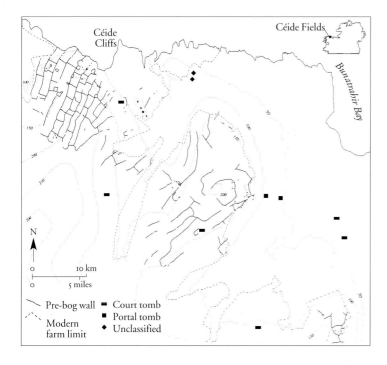

The Neolithic field system of Céide Fields, Co. Mayo, in northwest Ireland.

avoidance of marine foods. Nor can we determine whether the terrestrial foods consumed by these Neolithic people were from wild or domesticated resources so we cannot state that these populations had abandoned hunting and gathering and were now entirely dependent on domesticates. What these analyses do show, however, is that even in areas such as western Scotland that might be considered marginal or unsuitable for early agriculture, the Neolithic transition was not a gradual process, but a sudden change.

Monuments and the Neolithic

Some fifty years ago, it was thought that the idea of building megalithic tombs had been brought to Britain by settlers or even 'apostles of the megalithic faith' from neighbouring areas of Europe. Thirty years later, a rather different model had come to prevail, which emphasized the indigenous origins of monument types. Since the 1970s, some archaeologists have argued that the Neolithic monuments of Britain and Ireland were entirely home-grown, and this is certainly suggested by the presence here of monument types – henges and cursus monuments, for instance – that have no known parallels on the Continent of Europe. Most archaeologists today, however, consider that the examples found in Britain and Ireland form part of a broad west European family of Neolithic monuments based around a network of interregional contacts. What is particularly striking is that monuments and cereal agriculture appear together in these islands at around 4000 BC.

Several of the earliest secure Neolithic radiocarbon dates in Britain and Ireland come from chambered tombs, long mounds or other monuments. The majority fall in the period after 4000 BC, with the earliest reliable dates for unchambered long mounds in Yorkshire and southern England falling between 3800 and 3500 BC. Other monument types such as portal dolmens may be equally early. In Scotland, likewise, monuments such as the Pitnacree mortuary house belong to the very earliest stages of the Neolithic, around 4000 BC or the following few centuries. Thus the transition to the Neolithic appears in Britain and Ireland to have been marked by the construction of monuments almost from the very outset. The evidence suggests that there may have been a short initial period of two or three centuries, between 4000 BC and 3700 BC, when some of the earliest Neolithic communities created monuments of relatively modest scale, such as post settings, pavements, pits and small parallel banks. By around 3700 BC, however, much larger structures, including long mounds and causewayed camps, were being built.

Only a short interval in time thus appears to have separated the first domestic plants and animals and the earliest pottery from the

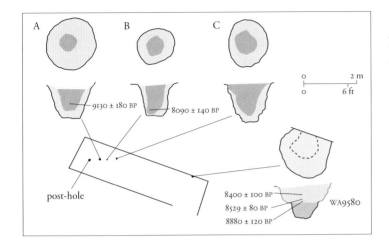

A B C

9130 ± 180 BP   8090 ± 140 BP

0   2 m

0   6 ft

post-hole

8400 ± 100 BP
8529 ± 80 BP   WA9580
8880 ± 120 BP

The row of Mesolithic post-holes discovered under the car park at Stonehenge.

first monuments. Many of these monuments would have been well within the capacities of small hunter-gatherer groups to build. Why, then, do monuments only appear after the Neolithic transition? It is true we can point to occasional evidence of Mesolithic monuments, such as the line of substantial post-holes dated to the 9th/8th millennium BC found in excavations beneath the car park at Stonehenge. But it is clear that for the most part, Mesolithic communities in Britain and Ireland did not create monuments, whereas Neolithic communities did. What was it that changed? In several parts of Britain and Ireland the numbers and densities of Neolithic monuments are so great as to demonstrate almost a compulsion to mould and model the landscape in this way. And that is what must lie behind the creation of Neolithic monuments: the development of a new world view, a new understanding of people's relationship to their surroundings and a new desire to materialize that relationship through the construction of chambered tombs, enclosures and stone circles.

Monuments in their social context

What kind of communities were they who built these cairns and circles? The settlement evidence is relatively sparse and does not suggest that the landscape of Britain and Ireland was heavily populated during the Neolithic period. Furthermore, whereas mention of Neolithic monuments may bring instantly to mind such grandiose structures as Stonehenge, Newgrange and Maes Howe, these sites are exceptional. Most Neolithic monuments are much smaller than this, and may have been built and extended by successive generations over many years. The majority of modest-sized chambered tombs and small stone circles could have been the work of individual communities comprising only a dozen or a couple of dozen individuals.

The larger Neolithic monuments, on the other hand, would have demanded a bigger work force. Several hundred individuals would have been required to shape and erect the stones used in the sarsen circle at Stonehenge, or indeed to move and manoeuvre the heavy capstones of some megalithic tombs. Yet even in these cases we lack any evidence for substantial Neolithic settlements. How then did these impressive and labour-demanding monuments come to be built by an essentially dispersed and small-scale population? The answer may be that they were the work of many small communities who came together for the purpose. If there were leaders, they have left no trace in the form of richly furnished burials: the latter appear only in the final centuries of the 3rd millennium BC, as the major period of monument-building was drawing to a close.

The larger Neolithic monuments were clearly sites of unusual significance, and must have been sacred places for the populations of the surrounding areas. Many of them have debris left from feasting. Hundreds of people may have converged seasonally on centres such as Brú na Bóinne (the Bend of the Boyne) and Stonehenge, for ceremonies that involved both communal meals, dancing, marriages, mortuary rituals, and the forging or reinforcing of alliances. Construction may sometimes have formed a part of these communal activities, since the building of the monuments was itself very likely a sacred act. Thus these need not have been highly centralized societies, with strong rulers controlling large work-forces, but they do testify to a powerful shared ideology, one that enabled enormous enterprises such as Knowth and Newgrange, Stonehenge 3 and Silbury Hill to be conceived and completed.

Landscape and monuments

The Neolithic monuments of Britain and Ireland were built of materials that were readily available, usually in a conspicuous form, in the local landscape. These materials might be timber and earth, or megalithic slabs. It is the megalithic monuments which of course have best survived the passage of time, but excavations at timber monuments have revealed how massive some of the timber elements would have been. Split oak trunks 1.5 m (5 ft) across such as were used in the Haddenham long mound in Cambridgeshire were truly monumental in scale, and as massive as many megalithic slabs.

Long-distance movement of the materials needed to build these monuments was relatively uncommon, though there are within Britain and Ireland a number of famous exceptions to this. The Boyne valley passage tombs incorporated stone which came from a considerable distance: white quartz from the Wicklow mountains 40 km (25 miles) to the south; dark grey granite and granodiorite from Dundalk

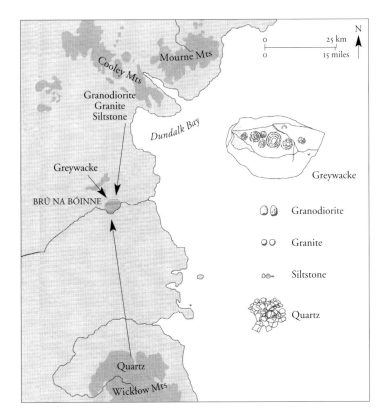

Sources of the stones used in the chambered tombs of Brú na Bóinne (Boyne valley), Co. Meath, in western Ireland.

Bay 35 km (22 miles) to the northeast. Still more spectacular was the transport of megalithic slabs to Stonehenge. The massive 40-tonne sarsens had been brought 30 km (19 miles) from the Marlborough Downs to the north; the smaller bluestones, each weighing around 1.5 tonnes, from the Preseli Hills of southwest Wales, a distance of some 240 km (150 miles). Claims that the bluestones may have reached the Stonehenge area as a result of glacial action during the last Ice Age have not so far found strong geological support: human transport remains the most probable explanation.

As mentioned, however, such instances of long-distance megalithic transport are exceptional, and most of the materials used to build the Neolithic monuments of Britain and Ireland came from the immediate vicinity. Where megalithic slabs are concerned, the nature of the local geology often imposed a distinctive shape and character on the monuments built from them. Thus the stone circles of Brodgar and Stenness on Orkney are memorable for their tall thin uprights of Orkney flagstone, with angular pointed tops, that follow the natural cleavage pattern of this material. On the small Scottish island of Arran, the tomb of Carn Ban incorporates megalithic blocks of contrasting geology and colour that come from different parts of the island.

15

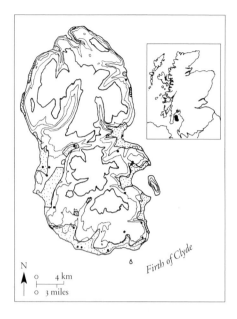

N

0   4 km

0   3 miles

Firth of Clyde

Few of the megalithic slabs used in these monuments have been intentionally shaped, and the use of unmodified natural blocks reinforces the close link between the built structures and the local landscape and geology. In some cases, indeed, the monuments may have been intentionally modelled to resemble local landscape features. The boulder burials of Ireland and the 'outcrop sites' of southwest Wales use natural slabs with minimal modification, merely propping them up to create a burial space beneath. These examples suggest that the inspiration for megalithic monuments may have arisen from the special significance accorded to natural rock outcrops, some of which may have been regarded as sacred sites. At Drumirril in Ireland, for instance, a rock outcrop decorated with panels of carvings was encircled by a Neolithic bank and ditch,

Above The Isle of Arran off the west coast of Scotland: black dots mark the location of megalithic tombs; stippling indicates the geological extent of red sandstones.

Right Cup-marks and concentric rings carved on a rock outcrop at Drumirril, Co. Monaghan, Ireland, probably in the Neolithic period.
Below Plan of the Neolithic chambered tomb of Carn Barn, Arran, and a cross-section through the chamber indicating the geological origins of the stones: red sandstones (stippled); granites and schists (blank).

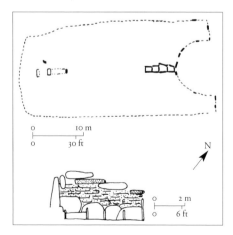

0   10 m

0   30 ft

N

0   2 m

0   6 ft

underscoring its special significance. It would be only a short step from this kind of practice to the pulling together of natural slabs to build megalithic monuments.

Yet persuasive though this argument may be, it cannot explain the whole of the Neolithic monument phenomenon. It does not, for example, account for the long linear cursus monuments, nor the unchambered long mounds, nor indeed the stone and timber circles and henges. Timber circles may have arisen from a tradition of

The Ring of Brodgar stone circle, Orkney, Scotland.

17

ceremonial spaces set in forest clearings; stone circles may imitate other ceremonial spaces among boulder scatters on rocky uplands, but their regularity suggests that they were meant to stand out and mark special places in a conspicuous way. Furthermore, many of the megalithic chambered tombs seem more to utilize elements of the local landscape (in the form of earth and boulders) than consciously to imitate features of it. Nobody could mistake Newgrange for a natural hill. Nonetheless, it remains likely that the form of these monuments was inspired by the nature and significance of the materials of which they were made.

Aside from the specific materials, the relationship of these Neolithic monuments to their landscape merits close attention. It is clear, for example, that different categories of monument are often placed in different types of location. In Ireland, passage tombs are found on prominent hills and ridges, whereas court cairns and portal tombs were built in lower-lying locations. The hilltop passage tombs were further away from the zones of everyday activity, and this intentional displacement must relate in some way to their prehistoric

Chambered tombs of the Carrowkeel cemetery, Co. Sligo, Ireland.

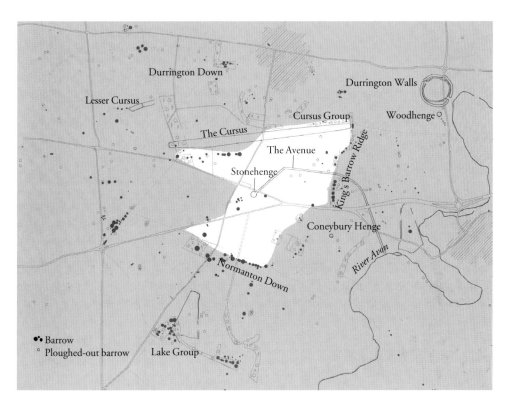

Durrington Down

Durrington Walls

Lesser Cursus

Cursus Group

Woodhenge

The Cursus

King's Barrow Ridge

The Avenue

Stonehenge

Coneybury Henge

Normanton Down

River Avon

•• Barrow
○ Ploughed-out barrow   Lake Group

significance. In Britain, a contrast has been observed between the landscape settings of henge monuments and those of stone circles: the former, with their enclosing banks and ditches, are usually in lowland or valley floor locations; the latter in more open positions with extensive views. In some cases, the visibility of distant mountains may have been important in siting a tomb. In southwest Wales, for example, several megalithic tombs have views of the mountain of Carn Meini, which is not only a distinctive landmark but was also the source of material for polished stone axes. Ethnography indicates that mountains are often important in traditional systems of belief and may be places of sacred significance. Visibility between monuments may also have been important. This is especially evident in the Bronze Age, when round barrows were constructed in proximity to major Neolithic monuments such as Avebury and Stonehenge. At Stonehenge, they were built not in the immediate vicinity of the stone circle but on the low ridges that overlook the site a kilometre and more away. Here again, visibility – being within sight of a sacred place – appears to have been the crucial factor. These examples make clear that Neolithic monuments should not be studied as discrete, isolated entities, but as elements of a larger landscape that was both natural and cultural in character.

The visual envelope (in white) of Stonehenge in southwest England: the rows of Bronze Age barrows on the ridges should be noted, especially King Barrow Ridge to the east and Normanton Down to the south.

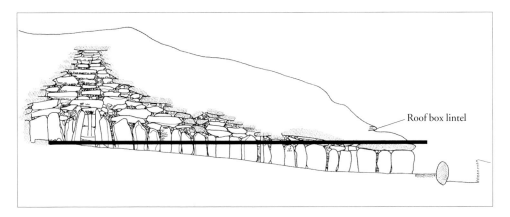

Roof box lintel

Cross-section through the chamber and passage of Newgrange: the horizontal line shows the path of the sun's rays at sunrise at the midwinter solstice, which penetrate the innermost part of the chamber.

Scanning the heavens

Neolithic people did not of course look only earthwards, but also raised their eyes to the heavens and observed the movements of the sun, moon and stars. The sky was as much a part of the setting of prehistoric monuments as was the land or (in some cases) the sea. It was William Stukeley in 1723 who first noted that the axis of Stonehenge was aligned with the midsummer sunrise. In doing so he initiated a trail of theory and speculation which has subsequently engulfed not only Stonehenge but also many other Neolithic monuments of Britain and Ireland, leading to claims for incredible and complex feats of astronomical observation and skill.

Many of these claims have been put forward by astronomers and engineers and have been rejected by most archaeologists since they are based on unlikely assumptions about the nature of the prehistoric societies of northwest Europe, and in some cases on faulty fieldwork. The only orientations that have found general acceptance are those concerning the sun. The daily passage of the sun and its regular variations throughout the year will have been well recognized by early prehistoric communities who used it to follow the changing seasons. The solstices – when sunrise and sunset reach their most northerly (summer) and most southerly (winter) point on the horizon in the northern hemisphere – may have been of especial significance. This much is suggested by the Neolithic monuments. Some, notably Stonehenge, appear to have been carefully aligned on the summer solstice sunrise, a feature that continues to draw people in their thousands to the site every year. Equally remarkable is the case of Newgrange in Ireland. The builders of this passage tomb carefully contrived an opening known as the 'roof box' above the passage entrance, which allows the sun's rays at dawn on the midwinter solstice to shine directly along the passage and illuminate the burial chamber at its far end. The intention may have been to invoke the symbolism of rebirth, as the sun reached its lowest and weakest point in the year before gaining in strength and height as the new year progressed. A similar alignment on the midwinter solstice sunrise direction has been noted at Maes Howe and Clava (and now has also been suggested for Stonehenge, see below, p. 122), so the phenomenon was not restricted to Ireland. Nonetheless, only a small minority of British and Irish megalithic tombs incorporate such orientations, and the question remains whether in some cases they could have arisen by chance. A cautionary tale is provided by Carn Ban on Arran. This chambered tomb faces northeast and appears to be accurately aligned on the midsummer solstice sunrise. There are, however, more than 20 other tombs of identical type on the same island, and their orientations span all points of the compass. There is hence no statistical demonstration that the choice of alignment at Carn Ban was governed by the position of the summer solstice.

It was during the 1960s and 1970s that the greatest number of theories about astronomical alignments among British and Irish megalithic monuments were put forward. They are especially associated with the name of Alexander Thom, who also argued that many stone circles had been laid out with geometrical precision according to a 'megalithic yard' of 0.829 m (2.7 ft). The irregular shape of the stones used in these monuments should have been sufficient in itself to warn against such exaggerated precision: most of the stones of these circles have irregular and unmodified profiles and surfaces, which is hardly what we would expect if they were intended to serve as accurate markers of distance. It is now more generally believed that the 'megalithic yard' corresponds to the average length of a human pace, and that these monuments may have been laid out simply by pacing out the ground. There is no reason, in any event, to believe

Orientations of the Neolithic chambered tombs on the Isle of Arran.

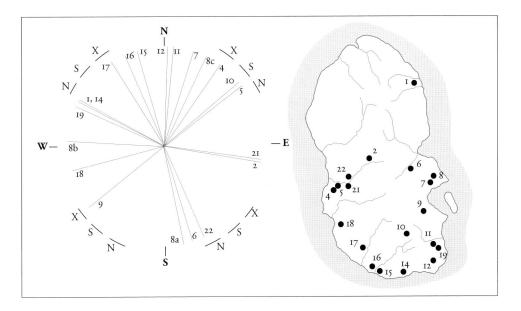

21

that the Neolithic builders were particularly concerned to achieve a high level of precision; that is a preoccupation more typical of modern engineers.

The same caution applies to many of the claims for solar, lunar and stellar orientations in stone circles and stone rows. Some of the stone rows of western Scotland and southwest Ireland may have been aligned on movements of the moon, but in other cases such claims have since been shown to be weak or erroneous. Most of the suggested orientations involve the direction of the point on the horizon at which the sun or moon rises or sets. Some sites, it is argued, are aligned on 'notches' between hills which mark the place (when seen from the monument) that the solar or lunar disk appears or disappears. These claims have proved difficult to substantiate. Prehistoric tree cover, long since lost, may have obscured many of the sight lines and would have altered the shape and height of the horizon. We are left with the dilemma that while, on the one hand, we can be reasonably confident that astronomical events will have been observed and will have been accorded significance by Neolithic communities, the attempt to demonstrate exactly which astronomical events were associated with which monuments is both difficult and hazardous.

The alignment of standing stones at Ballochroy, Argyll, Scotland, with the astronomical orientations proposed by Alexander Thom: to the northwest, towards the summer solstice sunset over Ben Corra; and to southwest, towards winter solstice sunset over Cara Island.

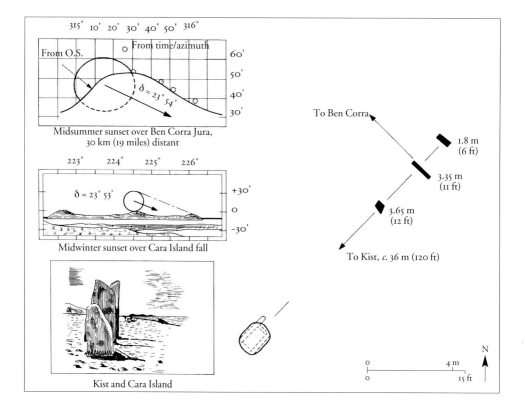

315° 10' 20' 30' 40' 50' 316°

From O.S.　From time/azimuth　60'

50'

δ = 23° 54'　40'

30'

Midsummer sunset over Ben Corra Jura,
30 km (19 miles) distant

223°　224°　225°　226°

δ = 23° 53'　+30'

0

-30'

Midwinter sunset over Cara Island fall

Kist and Cara Island

To Ben Corra

1.8 m
(6 ft)

3.35 m
(11 ft)

3.65 m
(12 ft)

To Kist, *c.* 36 m (120 ft)

N

0　　　　4 m

0　　　　15 ft

Death and the ancestors

In many of the Neolithic monuments of Britain and Ireland the presence of human bones links them to funerary practices. This is especially true of the numerous chambered cairns, or (in a slightly different sense) of the unchambered long barrows raised over the sites of timber mortuary houses. Burials are also frequently found at, or in association with, stone circles: the central cairn at Callanish, for example, or the peripheral cairn at Arbor Low, or the cremations in the bank and ditch of Stonehenge. The modern Western practice of separating the dead from the living may lead us to suppose therefore that these Neolithic monuments were part of a cult of the dead, or perhaps the veneration of ancestors.

To evaluate this argument we need to consider the broader issue of Neolithic burials. In first place, it is clear that Neolithic human remains are not only found at 'funerary' monuments, but also in other Neolithic contexts: in the shafts of flint mines, for example, or in the ditches of causewayed enclosures. To understand this better we must appreciate that remains of the dead may have been widely present in Neolithic societies, who did not separate them from the living in the way that has become familiar in recent centuries. Isolated human bones are found in Neolithic settlements and may have been curated by relatives of the dead. Furthermore, the mortuary structures of the earlier Neolithic – the chambered tombs and long mounds – appear to have been used not for the definitive disposal of corpses but for the temporary deposition of the dead body while the flesh decayed. Once that process was complete, the bones were often sorted and disturbed, and some of them withdrawn from the 'tomb' for disposal elsewhere or for keeping, perhaps, by relatives.

Aerial view of the stone circle at Callanish, Isle of Lewis, Scotland.

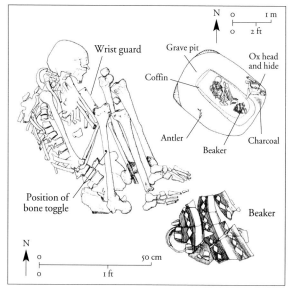

Top *Human skulls deposited in one of the side cells of the chambered tomb of Isbister, Orkney.*

Above *Late Neolithic single grave of Hemp Knoll, Wiltshire, accompanied by a Beaker vessel (crushed) placed at the foot of the corpse; around the body were traces of a probable wooden coffin; in one corner of the grave pit were the skull and hooves of a bovid – remains of an ox-hide.*

These practices led to the ultimate dismantling of the skeletons of the dead and the loss of skeletal integrity. Bones of different individuals were mixed together, as if the identity of the individual was no longer of significance once the flesh had decayed. Some have argued that this practice indicates that the dead entered the community of the 'ancestors', an anonymous group in which individual identity was no longer recognized. Towards the end of the Neolithic period, however, a change in burial practice occurs. Single graves, in which the skeleton was left intact and undisturbed, become more common. Individual identity was thus preserved in death, and along with this new practice goes the deposition in the grave of offerings or the belongings of the deceased. The dead were probably no longer anonymous. It is possible, indeed, that this change in burial practice represents a new way of reckoning descent, which henceforth laid emphasis not on the community of the ancestors but on specific individuals from whom goods or status were inherited. Thus burial mounds henceforth marked the graves of known and remembered individuals, from whom living relatives claimed descent, and from whom they may also have derived their status.

Viewed in the very broadest perspective, however, what is perhaps most striking about Neolithic burials is their relative scarcity. Neolithic communities may have been small in scale, but the recorded human remains are so few that it is still likely that many of the dead were disposed of in ways that have left no clear trace in the archaeological record. These may have included the disposal of corpses in rivers, if the 4th millennium BC date for a human skull found in the River Thames is significant. Rivers, seas, marshes and mountains may have been important in other ways too: as places of myth and legend, or the dwellings of the gods. The visible monuments – long mounds, chambered tombs, circles – must indeed be considered only part of a wider pattern of ritual and belief in Neolithic Britain and Ireland.

CHAPTER TWO

Scotland

SCOTLAND IS A LAND OF VARIED NATURAL TERRAIN. IN THE SOUTH AND east, lowland plains and undulating hill country provide good arable and grazing land. To north and west of these areas are the highlands, divided by the Great Glen which cuts the country transversely from Inverness to Fort William. Beyond again, on the northern and western fringes, lie the islands – Orkney and Shetland, Outer and Inner Hebrides. These geographical contrasts have had an impact on the nature of the prehistoric monuments: stone is widely abundant, sometimes in the form of boulders or megalithic slabs, in the north and west, while earth and timber were extensively employed in the lowland areas. This mixture of materials characterizes the Neolithic monuments of Scotland just as it does those of southern Britain and Ireland, and there are more formal similarities, too, between the types of monument found in these different regions. It is important, however, to avoid imposing a single blueprint on the Neolithic monuments of Britain and Ireland, since each region presents its own distinctive developments.

Earth and timber monuments

The earliest Neolithic monuments of the lowland zone of Scotland appear to have been of timber, or earth and timber. One of the earliest such monuments, and also one of the largest, is the Cleaven Dyke in Perthshire. This consists of a central bank, up to 15 m (50 ft) wide and almost 2 m (6.5 ft) high, flanked by parallel ditches 40–50 m (130–165 ft) apart, that runs in an approximately straight line for almost 2 km (1.25 miles). Without the central bank it would be classed as a cursus. Investigation has shown that the Cleaven Dyke was constructed in segments, beginning from the northwest end, the first element being an oval burial mound of a type known elsewhere in the region. To this was added a 'tail' in the form of a narrow, 80-m (262 ft) long mound, which was subsequently extended in stages to produce the linear monument we see today. Radiocarbon dates for charcoal beneath the

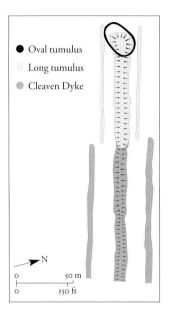

- ● Oval tumulus
- ▦ Long tumulus
- ● Cleaven Dyke

N

| 0 | 50 m |
| 0 | 150 ft |

Left *Northwestern terminal of the Cleaven Dyke, Perthshire: the oval mound represents the first phase, followed by the long tumulus and then by the Cleaven Dyke itself.* Below *Reconstruction of the Cleaven Dyke at the beginning of the 4th millennium BC.*

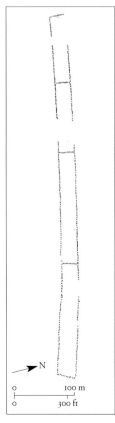

N

| 0 | 100 m |
| 0 | 300 ft |

Milton of Guthrie, Angus: a 600-m (1968-ft) long linear monument defined by post-holes and with internal divisions.

Cleaven Dyke fall within the range 4750–4000 BC, but the monument itself probably began with the construction of the oval mound at its northwestern end early in the 4th millennium BC.

In the area to the east of the Cleaven Dyke, long linear monuments defined by parallel lines of post-holes have been traced on aerial photographs. These are perhaps the timber equivalents of the Cleaven Dyke and attain similar (if not quite the same) dimensions: the example at Milton of Guthrie measures 600 m (1968 ft) long and is divided into four sections by a series of cross-walls. Linear structures such as these illustrate the scale of monumental construction undertaken even in the very earliest centuries of the Scottish Neolithic. They cut across the landscape, forming barriers to movement. Monuments such as the Cleaven Dyke are a remarkable testimony to the change that occurred with the transition to the Neolithic; nothing remotely like it survives from the preceding Mesolithic period. These monuments were, furthermore, associated with new attitudes to death and burial.

The oval barrow beneath the northwest terminal of the Cleaven Dyke has not been excavated, but may be compared with the mortuary structure at Pitnacree, some 25 km (15 miles) to the west. This began as a pair of massive timber posts set 3 m (10 ft) apart, joined by side-walls of less substantial (possibly wickerwork) construction. It was in fact a mortuary house similar in design and construction to those known from southern Britain at Street House, Fussell's Lodge or in the first phase of Wayland's Smithy (p. 78). Like those southern examples, the Pitnacree mortuary house was subsequently burned. A new mortuary chamber was built directly over the remains, with stone-paved floor and turf and timber walls, entered by a stone-built passage at one end. This second chamber contained evidence of four cremation burials and was incorporated within an oval cairn of turf and stone. Timber mortuary houses have also been found beneath chambered cairns in southwest Scotland. At Lochhill, for example, a narrow elongated timber structure was supported by massive timber posts at either end, with two further intermediate posts. A low wall of granite blocks was built to a height of 0.3 m (1 ft) around this mortuary chamber,

Oval mound of Pitnacree, Perthshire, enclosing a turf and timber mortuary chamber surrounded by stone blocks, with stone-paved floor.

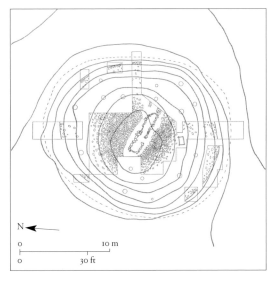

N ←

0   10 m

0   30 ft

Below *Conjectural reconstruction of the initial Pitnacree mortuary structure with wickerwork side-walls and massive end-posts – here imagined carved into a roughly anthropomorphic shape.*

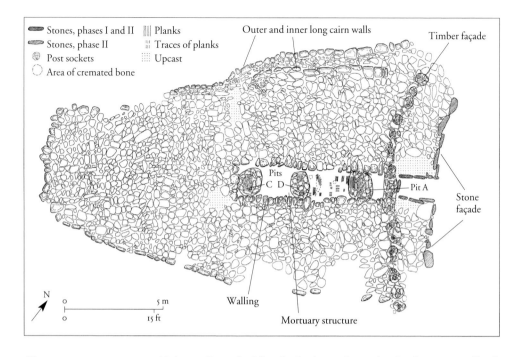

Stones, phases I and II
Stones, phase II
Post sockets
Area of cremated bone
Planks
Traces of planks
Upcast

Outer and inner long cairn walls
Timber façade
Pits
C D
Pit A
Stone façade
N
0   5 m
0   15 ft
Walling
Mortuary structure

The mortuary structure at Lochhill was originally constructed of massive timber posts, with a floor of oak planks and a slightly concave façade of tree trunks. This structure was subsequently burned before being incorporated into a cairn furnished with a concave façade of stone blocks and an axial chamber.

which was floored with oak planks, as shown by the fragments of bark that survived. It too contained cremations like the Pitnacree structure, and was intentionally burned down before the chambered cairn was built over it. Wood from one of the planks gave a radiocarbon date of between 4250 and 3500 BC. A similar mortuary house has recently been excavated at Eweford Cottages south of Dunbar, with early or mid-4th millennium pottery, and in that instance the site was abandoned after use, rather than monumentalized as at Lochhill by the construction of a mound or cairn.

These sites illustrate the practice of collective burial – the remains of several individuals placed together – and the use of fire to transform the bodies of the dead. The cremations must have taken place elsewhere, and the remains then laid to rest in these mortuary houses. The final act seems to have been the destruction by fire of the mortuary house itself, though this was often followed by the raising of a mound or cairn.

In eastern Scotland, timber mortuary houses sometimes underlie unchambered long mounds. These mounds form part of a widespread tradition extending from Caithness to Dorset. The most famous Scottish example is at Dalladies, near Montrose, a 50-m (165-ft) long turf mound with out-turned horns at the eastern end. The edges of the mound were held in place by a dry-stone kerb, outside which shallow flanking ditches were cut into the gravel subsoil. This mound covered the remains of a timber mortuary house similar to those at Lochhill and Pitnacree. In an intermediate stage, however, this had been replaced by a rectangular dry-stone enclosure, with an entrance at the northwest, that had been covered by a lightly built timber superstructure roofed by bark. The timber elements were burned before the long mound was built, some time in the second half of the 4th millennium BC. What was especially surprising about the Dalladies mortuary house was that it was not placed axially, in line with the horns at the eastern end of the later long mound. Instead it lay obliquely under the northern flank; thus when the long mound was built, it was decided to place it on an entirely different axis from the mortuary house that it was to cover. Was the mound always part of the plan, or was it added as an afterthought? The change in orientation suggests that the latter is more likely. Hence, once again it appears that mortuary houses were not just the first stages in long mound construction, but had their own separate symbolism and significance.

Alongside timber mortuary houses and linear monuments are two other categories of early timber structure: circles and houses. An early timber circle has been excavated at Temple Wood in the Kilmartin Valley of Mid Argyll, where a ring of substantial timber posts some 10 m (33 ft) in diameter was subsequently dismantled and replaced by a stone circle. The replacement of the initial timber structure may have been intended to monumentalize the original sacred setting and give it a durable, permanent form. It is possible that as the timber uprights rotted they were removed and the stones raised in their place. A second, larger stone circle was later built alongside. The Temple Wood stone circle dates to the 4th millennium BC and its timber predecessor to perhaps the first half of that millennium.

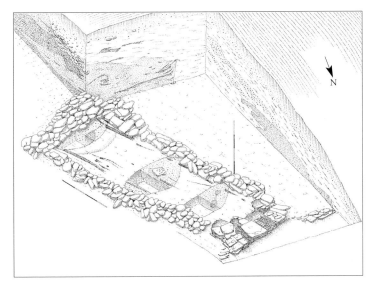

The 'mortuary house' of Dalladies: a structure with three massive timber posts was replaced by a rectangular enclosure with dry-stone walls, which was then burned and hidden beneath the northern edge of a long mound constructed of turf on a different axis.

Later Scottish timber circles were larger in scale. At North Mains in Perthshire, on the edge of the highland zone, a flat-bottomed ditch with external bank enclosed a setting of 24 timber posts in the form of a circle some 26 m (85 ft) across. The arrangement of a ditch with external bank and single entrance associates this with the henge monuments of southern Britain. North Mains was, however, a relatively small and simple henge compared with Balfarg some 40 km (25 miles) to the east. Here a ditch and bank encircled a much larger area, 65 m (213 ft) in diameter, containing a whole series of concentric timber circles, plus one or possibly two rings of standing stones. Once again, an initially timber monument appears to have been rebuilt in stone.

Finally, within the category of timber ceremonial monuments we should perhaps include a rather different type of site: a group of large Neolithic timber houses. The most famous of these is at Balbridie, near Aberdeen, an apparently solitary timber building measuring 24 by 12 m (78 by 40 ft). From its size and shape it was at first thought to be an Iron Age structure, but radiocarbon dates demonstrated that it had been built during the 4th millennium BC and hence belonged to the earlier Neolithic. Large quantities of wheat and barley were recovered during the excavation, and these show that cereals must have been handled within the building, but there was no chaff from the processing of the crops and there were no storage pits. The Balbridie Neolithic house was such an unexpected discovery that some have doubted whether it was really a domestic dwelling. Yet another large timber hall, measuring 25 by 9 m (82 by 39.5 ft), was recently exca-

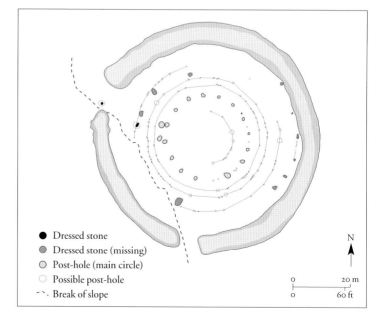

The henge monument of Balfarg, Fife: the circular ditch enclosed two rings of standing stones, as well as a primary timber circle marked by post-holes. More post-holes belonging to several additional timber circles have also been located.

● Dressed stone
◉ Dressed stone (missing)
○ Post-hole (main circle)
○ Possible post-hole
- - - Break of slope

N

0   20 m
0   60 ft

vated at Claish Farm near Stirling, and a third has been found at Crathes, opposite Balbridie. Are these simply houses, or did they have a ceremonial function? The debate is ongoing, but the lack of crop-processing debris at Balbridie may suggest it was a place of feasting rather than an everyday farmstead. The grain may have been cleaned elsewhere, at domestic sites, before it was brought to the 'house'. Claish is still more unusual since it lacks stone tools. This absence may, once again, be incompatible with the notion of domestic activity. These roofed structures of the early 4th millennium BC are followed later in the millennium by similar post-built structures that were almost certainly unroofed, including Littleour and Whitmuirhaugh. Thus long houses may have been followed by oblong ceremonial post-settings, reinforcing the symbolic quality of the houses which may have been as much timber monuments as dwellings of Scotland's 4th millennium inhabitants.

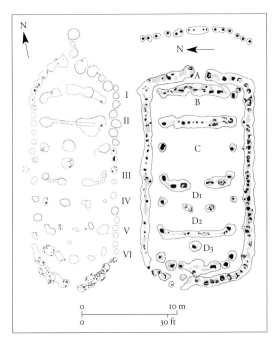

Neolithic long houses of Claish Farm (left) and Balbridie (right).

Southwest Scotland

While timber and earth played a major role in eastern Scotland, in the west and north stone construction predominated in the form either of dry-stonework or megalithic slabs, or the two together. These are the areas of the classic Scottish chambered tombs and stone circles, from southwest Scotland through Argyll and the Hebrides to Caithness and Orkney.

The chambered tombs of southwest Scotland are conventionally divided into two principal types: Clyde cairns and Bargrennan passage graves. Recent excavations have shown that these sites often have complex histories. At Mid Gleniron I, for example, the sequence began with two small oval chambered cairns, placed in line one behind the other. Subsequently, they were both incorporated into a single long cairn with a deep concave façade – a classic Clyde cairn. One of the most impressive Clyde cairns in this region is Cairnholy I, some 43 m (140 ft) in length by 10 m (33 ft) wide, with a concave façade of thin uprights – almost like flagpoles or totem poles – flanking the narrow entrance to a simple elongated megalithic box divided into two compartments, the rearmost closed off by a slab. This is a

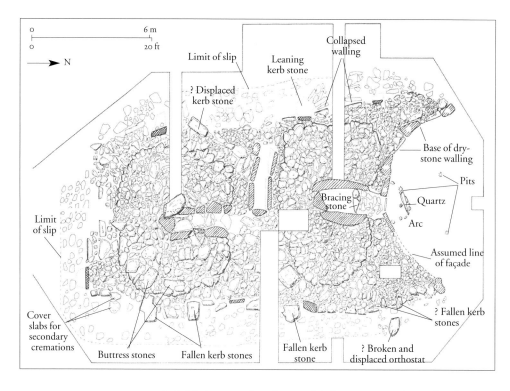

The following labels appear on the plan:

6 m / 20 ft

N

Limit of slip

? Displaced kerb stone

Leaning kerb stone

Collapsed walling

Base of dry-stone walling

Pits

Quartz

Bracing stone

Arc

Limit of slip

Assumed line of façade

Cover slabs for secondary cremations

Buttress stones

Fallen kerb stones

Fallen kerb stone

? Broken and displaced orthostat

? Fallen kerb stones

The cairn of Mid Gleniron I: two small oval monuments, each with its own burial chamber, have been incorporated into a larger cairn with a semicircular façade to the north and a third chamber opening on its western flank.

typical Clyde-type chamber, and it is easy to envisage the development of such chambers from timber mortuary houses like that found beneath the Lochhill cairn (which is also in this region). Indeed, at Lochhill the subsequent long cairn that was built over the timber mortuary chamber itself contains just such a Clyde-type chamber.

Bargrennan tombs, by contrast, are passage graves beneath small circular or oval cairns. They differ from Clyde cairns not only in their shape and size, but also their locations. Bargrennan tombs are frequently found in isolated upland basins amongst natural mounds and hillocks. Clyde cairns, by contrast, tend to be located around the lower-lying coastal zone, often with views of the sea. The two tomb types may have been contemporary, perhaps used by the same communities at different times of the year or for different kinds of ceremonies involving the dead. It is also possible, however, that the Bargrennan tombs are somewhat later in date.

Opposite above *Distribution of Neolithic chambered tombs on Arran and the adjacent mainland of southwestern Scotland in relation to areas of arable land on the mainland and to the distribution of Neolithic polished stone axes.*

Opposite below *Orthostatic façade of the Clyde cairn of Cairnholy I.*

Argyll and Arran

To the north, Clyde cairns are one of the principal Neolithic monument types in Argyll. The example at Monamore on Arran yielded a particularly early date (4220–3660 BC), though this was associated with activity in the forecourt rather than in the tomb itself. The mountainous island of Arran is especially rich in chambered tombs, with some 22 Clyde cairns. One of the most famous is Carn Ban, where the careful alternation of differently coloured stone (p. 16)

draws attention to the use of materials from two different parts of the island: grey-white schist for the orthostats of the passage and chamber and for the façade; red sandstone for the drystonework above the orthostats and for the body of the cairn; and the two materials in alternation for the capstones and the kerb. As mentioned above, Carn Ban is also notable for the orientation of its passage and chamber, which are aligned very closely on the midsummer solstice sunrise. The 21 other Clyde cairns on Arran face in a wide range of compass directions, however (p. 21), and the

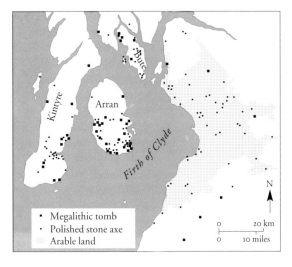

- Megalithic tomb
- Polished stone axe
- Arable land

Kintyre · Bute · Arran · Firth of Clyde

N

0   20 km

0   10 miles

likely conclusion is that the Carn Ban alignment is the result merely of coincidence.

The distribution of tombs on Arran has been used (as has that on Rousay: see below) to develop a particular model of early Neolithic communities in which each small farming settlement had its own tomb that was located close to a patch of arable land. The positioning of the Arran tombs was held to indicate a segmented pattern of land division, which went hand-in-hand with an egalitarian society. This interpretation assumes that the island was a relatively isolated, self-contained social world. Consideration of the broader geographical context suggests otherwise. Arran stands within a deep marine inlet framed by the peninsula of Kintyre to the west and the mainland of Strathclyde to the east. Chambered cairns are more common on the islands of Bute and Arran and on the Kintyre peninsula than on the mainland to the east, yet the main focus of settlement in the region appears to have been in Strathclyde. Bute, Arran and Kintyre may have been marginal areas during the earlier Neolithic and were perhaps exploited on only a seasonal basis. Thus, in locating the chambered cairns in these less settled areas, the communities may have been placing the dead at the margins of the land of the living. The mountains of Arran, rising impressively towards the sky, give it a special aura, and make it a visual focus for the whole surrounding region. It is perhaps not surprising that it became a favoured burial place.

The pear-shaped cairn at Achnacreebeag, Argyll, encloses two small megalithic chambers; that to the northwest was perhaps at the centre of an original circular cairn which was subsequently extended to accommodate the second chamber.

Arran was also centrally located in relation to maritime activity. The island was the source of the glassy black pitchstone used like flint to make stone tools. Arran pitchstone is found on the adjacent mainland and travelled even further afield to northern Ireland. Connections across the narrow seas to Ireland may have been particularly close. Antrim flint and polished stone axes of Irish porcellanite reached southwest Scotland, and there are similarities too in the tomb traditions, with Clyde cairns and Irish court cairns sharing several features, notably the concave façade and the segmented, box-like chamber.

Still longer-distance connections have been suggested for a tomb to the north of Arran, at Achnacreebeag, near Oban. This was a two-phase

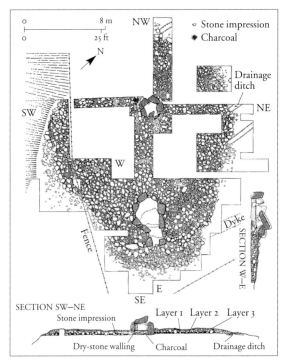

SECTION SW–NE
Stone impression
Dry-stone walling   Charcoal   Drainage ditch
Layer 1 Layer 2 Layer 3

8 m
25 ft
NW
N
SW
W
NE
Stone impression
Charcoal
Drainage ditch
Dyke
SECTION W–E
Fence
E
SE

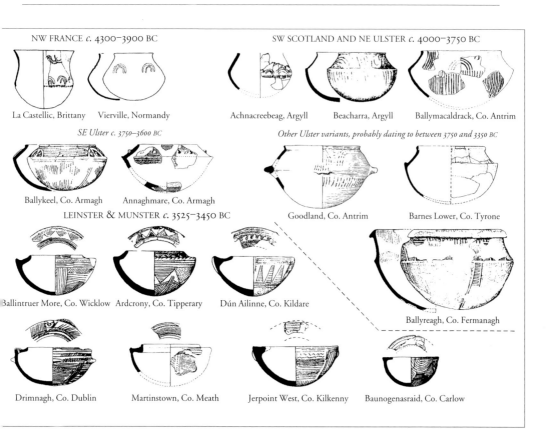

NW FRANCE *c.* 4300–3900 BC

La Castellic, Brittany   Vierville, Normandy

SW SCOTLAND AND NE ULSTER *c.* 4000–3750 BC

Achnacreebeag, Argyll   Beacharra, Argyll   Ballymacaldrack, Co. Antrim

SE Ulster c. 3750–3600 BC

Ballykeel, Co. Armagh   Annaghmare, Co. Armagh

Other Ulster variants, probably dating to between 3750 and 3350 BC

Goodland, Co. Antrim   Barnes Lower, Co. Tyrone

LEINSTER & MUNSTER *c.* 3525–3450 BC

Ballintruer More, Co. Wicklow   Ardcrony, Co. Tipperary   Dún Ailinne, Co. Kildare

Ballyreagh, Co. Fermanagh

Drimnagh, Co. Dublin   Martinstown, Co. Meath   Jerpoint West, Co. Kilkenny   Baunogenasraid, Co. Carlow

monument with two separate burial chambers. It began as a circular cairn 18 m (60 ft) in diameter around a central chamber formed by five uprights and a large capstone. The chamber had been sealed once the capstone was in place and the cairn had been built around it. This simple megalithic monument was later enlarged by the construction of a passage grave backing against the southeastern edge of the cairn, which was extended to cover it, thus producing a pear-shaped monument. The passage grave had a short passage leading to a polygonal chamber, a form which is also known in the Hebrides, though it is relatively uncommon in mainland Argyll. Amongst the pottery from the passage grave was a carinated bowl of a type named after the chambered cairn of Beacharra in Kintyre. This vessel was decorated with an incised pattern of nested arcs above the carination, and a short row of vertical lines below. Parallels can be drawn with Neolithic pottery from northeast Ireland, but the Achnacreebeag vessel has recently been compared also with French Neolithic pottery of 'Castellic' style, such as that from the passage grave of Vierville in Normandy. Fragments of two other vessels in the Achnacreebeag passage grave have also been claimed to have close French parallels, leading to the idea

Pottery parallels between northwest France (Castellic, Vierville), southwest Scotland (Achnacreebeag, Beacharra) and Ireland during the 4th millennium BC.

that there was direct contact between western Scotland and northwest France in the late 5th or early 4th millennium BC, a Neolithic forerunner, perhaps, of the 'auld alliance' between France and Scotland in the 16th century AD. If the passage grave at Achnacreebeag dates to around 4000 BC, then the closed central chamber must be earlier still, and could qualify as one of the first megalithic monuments in western Scotland.

This example has the merit of emphasizing the interregional connections that must have operated during the Neolithic period. Such connections are given solid form by the movements of polished stone axes and other raw materials referred to earlier. The study of British prehistory has all too often assumed that the sea was a barrier, and an obstacle to contact, whereas historical records frequently show quite the opposite. Less than 25 km (16 miles) of open sea separates the Mull of Kintyre from the Antrim coast of northern Ireland, and boats may regularly have plied the seaways connecting Ireland with Argyll. Similarities in monument forms or material culture between the two regions should therefore hardly come as a surprise. But whether we should envisage direct connections over much larger distances – between Argyll and Brittany, for example – is less certain.

The Western Isles

Nowhere would maritime contact have been more important than in the island archipelagos of western and northern Scotland: the Inner and Outer Hebrides in the west, the Orkney and Shetland Isles to the north. The Inner Hebrides lie close to the Scottish mainland and were certainly occupied in the Mesolithic: shell middens excavated on Oronsay have been dated to between 6200 and 5400 BC, and there were others on Skye, off the coast of Mull, and on the Scottish mainland. The midden at Sand on the mainland facing Skye has dates going back to 7600 BC. Given the maritime setting, one might have expected the exploitation of marine resources (fish, shellfish, sea mammals) to have continued into the Neolithic period, but as noted, recent analysis of the isotopic composition of human bone suggests otherwise. Instead, there is a distinct and relatively sudden switch at the beginning of the Neolithic away from marine resources (which had played such an important part in the Mesolithic diet) to an exclusive reliance on terrestrial resources. These probably included the newly introduced domesticates: wheat and barley, sheep, cattle and pig.

Further to the west, the Outer Hebrides are separated from the rest of Scotland by much wider expanses of more difficult water, but recent evidence shows that they too were settled during the Mesolithic period. The Outer Hebrides also have a series of Neolithic monuments, notably a number of passage graves which form a distinct cluster on the island of North Uist. This, like Arran, may have been a land of the dead. The most famous megalithic site of the Outer Hebrides, however, is undoubtedly the complex of stone circles, rows and a chambered cairn at Callanish on the west coast of Lewis, the largest of the Outer Hebrides.

The setting is spectacular: a promontory rising steeply above the shores of Loch Roag, one of the few deep and sheltered marine inlets on this coast of the island. The main focus at Callanish is a cross-shaped arrangement of standing stones: rows of tall thin pillars of gneiss converging on a stone circle surrounding a chambered cairn. The stones themselves probably came from nearby coastal cliffs. The long northern arm of the cross, 83 m (272 ft) in length, is doubled on its eastern side by a second row, creating an avenue, but the shorter rows leading from the east, west and south of the central stone circle are (with the exception of a sole outlying stone) all single rows.

The circle itself consists of 13 unworked uprights arranged in a ring approximately 12 m (40 ft) in diameter. At the centre stands a single taller stone, 5.8 m (19 ft) high. An open ring with central upright may have been the original intention, but shortly afterwards a chambered cairn was inserted within the stone circle, a simple stalled example with its entrance facing east. Circle and cairn have together been dated to between 2900 and 2600 BC.

Callanish is not alone in this region: there are half a dozen more stone circles around the shores of Loch Roag, and others on the neighbouring Hebridean island of North Uist. The North Uist circles are much larger than those of Callanish, with several of them approaching 40 m (130 ft) in diameter. It is perhaps surprising to find such a cluster of monuments in such a relatively outlying region, and we may wonder whether they were focal points for communities from a wider area. Their very remoteness may have added to their aura as places set apart from everyday life, in distant sacred landscapes. Did maritime pilgrims visit the stone circles at certain times of year, or for special ceremonies? The islands themselves can never have supported a large population in prehistory.

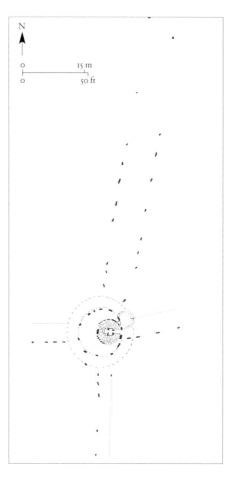

Plan of the central complex of Callanish on the Isle of Lewis, with a stone circle and radiating lines of standing stones; the passage grave in its small circular cairn was added within the circle a few centuries later.

Orkney

Rounding the northwest tip of mainland Scotland, the Atlantic seaways bring us to the Orkney islands, and one of the most remarkable collections of megalithic monuments in Britain. These islands are separated from the Scottish mainland by less than 15 km (9.5 miles) of open sea, but the straits (known as the Pentland Firth) are often rough and the crossing is not always as comfortable as the short distance might promise. Up to 14,000 years ago, what are now islands were joined to the Scottish mainland (and to each other) by a low-lying plain. It was the melting of the ice sheets and consequent rise in sea-level which made Orkney a cluster of around 40 islands, large and small, plus a number of isolated rocks. They were first visited in the Late Mesolithic period, perhaps by occasional fishing expeditions. Good evidence for permanent settlement begins only in the Neolithic period, during the 4th millennium BC.

The cairn that covers the passage grave of Maes Howe on Orkney is located on a platform surrounded by a circular bank and rock-cut ditch, possibly the remains of a henge that preceded the construction of the chambered burial mound.

The most famous of all Orkney monuments is Maes Howe, a large and impressive passage grave with regular cruciform ground plan covered by a soaring corbelled vault, the whole executed in the smooth-splitting Orkney flagstone that produces such a remarkable appearance. The chamber is entered through a passage 7 m (23 ft) long, each of its walls formed by a massive monolith placed on its side. At the outer end, a niche in one of the side walls holds an upright slab which was originally drawn forward to block the passage entrance.

Entering the chamber for the first time is one of the most memorable experiences offered by British megalithic monuments, as the confined dimensions of the passage open out into the tall corbel-vaulted space beyond, some 3.8 m (12.5 ft) high (although its upper part has been destroyed). At each corner of the chamber stands a large upright monolith, while directly facing the passage, and to both sides of the chamber, regular rectangular openings give access to small side cells. These are raised above ground level, and access to them was blocked by square stone plugs.

Of the contents of Maes Howe, alas, little survived to be discovered when the first archaeologists entered the tomb (via the roof) in 1861. There were no human remains, save for a

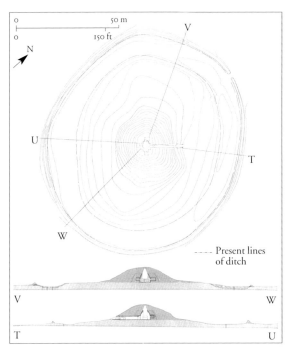

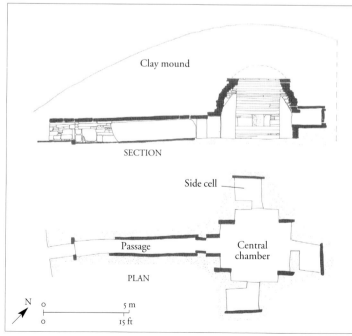

Clay mound

SECTION

Side cell

Passage

Central chamber

PLAN

N

0   5 m

0   15 ft

Above *The cairn of Maes Howe with its surrounding embankment.*

Left *On three sides of the quadrangular chamber of Maes Howe a rectangular opening gives access to a side cell. Both walls of the passage consist of a single massive longitudinal slab: these may be re-used standing stones.*

Interior of the chamber at Maes Howe looking out, and (opposite above) faint carved lines discovered in the chamber of Maes Howe which may have been guidelines for painted decoration.

single skull fragment in one of the side-cells. It soon became clear, indeed, that these Victorian archaeologists were not the first people to re-enter the tomb since the prehistoric builders closed it. Some 33 runic inscriptions had been carved on the chamber walls by a party (or several parties) of Norsemen in the 1150s. These make reference to a 'great treasure' that had been carried off from the tomb, though this can hardly be a reference to the original Neolithic deposits, and may simply have been a legend of buried wealth. Or had the tomb been reused for the burial of a Norse chieftain when Orkney was conquered by the Vikings in the 9th century? There is evidence that the encircling bank around the mound was heightened at about that time. The Maes Howe bank and the ditch that accompany it are in origin Neolithic, however, and are a unique feature of this tomb. No other Neolithic chambered tomb on Orkney has an encircling bank and ditch. This provides an important clue to the history and development of the monument. Excavations in 1995 behind the chamber discovered the socket for a former standing stone on the platform between the mound and the ditch, and it is possible that Maes Howe originated as a henge or stone circle. The massive stone slabs that form the side-walls of the passage and the monoliths at the corners of the chamber may all have been parts of this earlier stone setting. The Maes Howe we visit today may therefore have been built within the bank and ditch of an earlier stone circle whose massive monolithic uprights were re-employed in the construction of the passage grave. Maes Howe thus takes its place alongside the many other examples of megalithic monuments – including Newgrange, Stonehenge and Bryn Celli Ddu – that underwent radical remodelling during their Neolithic use.

A recent discovery leads us to believe that the chamber of Maes Howe, along with other chambered tombs of Neolithic Orkney, originally had painted decoration. Fine lines, scarcely visible to the naked eye, may have been guidelines for motifs and panels of painted decoration on the walls of the chamber.

The Stones of Stenness, Orkney: the parallel-sided standing stones with their angular tops illustrate the characteristic fracture patterns of Orkney flagstone.

The appearance of Maes Howe in its stone circle phase can easily be envisaged from the two neighbouring monuments which have survived as stone circles: the Ring of Brodgar and the Stones of Stenness. Brodgar is the larger and better preserved, a ring of perhaps 60 stones, of which 22 still stand together with five fallen slabs and the stumps of a dozen more, within a rock-cut ditch 105 m (345 ft) in diameter and over 3 m (10 ft) deep. Stenness, on lower land closer to Maes Howe, is less than half the diameter of Brodgar and was largely demolished in the early 19th century. The surviving stones (plus some that were re-erected) provide an evocative illustration of the shape into which Orkney flagstone can be split, furnishing tall thin monoliths with regular faces, parallel sides and angular, pointed tops. The same shapes are found in the monoliths incorporated into the passage and chamber of Maes Howe.

While the standing stones and encircling ditches are the most prominent elements of Brodgar and Stenness, other features may lie buried within their perimeter. Excavations at the

Plan of the Stones of Stenness following excavations by Graham Ritchie which revealed the sockets of several standing stones that have now disappeared, along with a quadrangular central 'hearth' edged by massive slabs. Numbers 2, 3, 5, 7 are standing stones still surviving upright; 8, 10, 11 are stumps of broken standing stones; and 1, 6, 9 are the sockets of now-vanished stones.

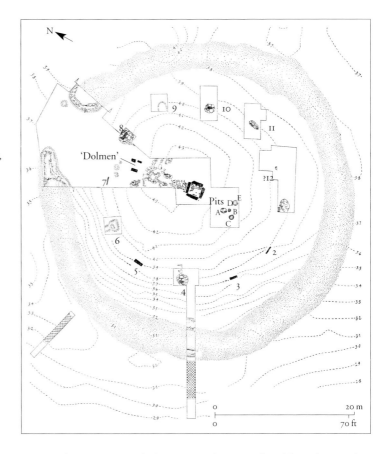

centre of Stenness revealed a rectangular stone-lined hearth, together with other stone- and post-holes. Fire, and indeed feasting, may have been an important part of the ceremonies carried out here. Potsherds with distinctive 'Grooved Ware' decoration have been found at Stenness and at other ceremonial sites as distant as Knowth and Newgrange in Ireland and Durrington Walls in southern England. At those sites – and more particularly at Durrington and Knowth – the large numbers of animal bones suggested that the consumption of roast pork may have been a key part of the activities.

The particular interest of Maes Howe, Brodgar and Stenness as individual sites is greatly enhanced when we consider their geographical proximity. They stand together in a key topographical area of the main island of Orkney, a place perhaps of special significance. The landscape here forms a lowland basin, fringed by mountains. Through the centre of this basin passes a narrow isthmus, flanked to either side by sea lochs. The monuments are grouped around this isthmus, Brodgar on slightly higher ground immediately to the west, Stenness and Maes Howe a short distance to the east. And these are not the only monuments in this complex. Beyond Brodgar on still higher ground is another circle, the Ring of Bookan, with ditch and bank, though apparently lacking standing stones. Beside the isthmus itself is the 6-m (20-ft) tall Watch Stone, while other isolated standing stones dot the hillsides round about. This inward-looking basin with its cluster of impressive monuments may have been considered as a kind of 'axis mundi' by Orkney Neolithic societies, a sacred and ritual focus at the heart of the archipelago of islands.

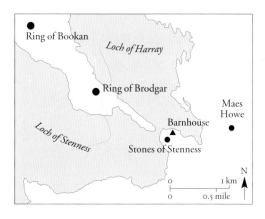

Above *The location of monuments around Maes Howe: stone circles of Brodgar and Stenness and the Neolithic settlement of Barnhouse.*

Below *Maes Howe and its surroundings in a watercolour of 1865; in the background can be seen, on the left, two of the standing stones of the Stones of Stenness, and to the right, on the sloping hillside, the Ring of Brodgar stone circle.*

43

Tombs and houses

Maes Howe, as we have seen, may have been built as a stone circle and only later altered to a passage grave. The cruciform plan of the Maes Howe chamber, however, has a very close local parallel in the Neolithic structures recently excavated at Barnhouse, near Stenness. This site contains the ground plans of 12 stone-built houses, each having a rectangular main room with furnishings arranged in cruciform manner: a square central hearth, a 'dresser' against the rear wall, and beds to either side, sometimes recessed into the side walls. One house (house 2) departs from the usual pattern, being both larger and more monumental than the others, and containing twin main rooms. Furthermore, the projecting inner corners formed quadrangular niches, much in the same way as in the Maes Howe burial chamber. Both in ground plan and certain constructional details, therefore, this Barnhouse structure echoes the Maes Howe chamber, though on a smaller scale. There are also parallels to be drawn between Barnhouse and the Stones of Stenness in the square central hearths and the circular shape of houses and stone circle. Thus what we appear to have in this limited geographical focus is a cluster of Neolithic structures linked together by features of ground plan and construction. Some of them (Barnhouse) were primarily domestic in character, others (Maes Howe) funerary, with stone circles (Stenness and Brodgar) providing loci perhaps for ritual gatherings and feasting, and the individual standing stones such as the Watch Stone marking out significant features or boundaries within the landscape.

Parallels between the design of houses and tombs on Orkney can be extended to other sites. The Orkney chambered tombs number

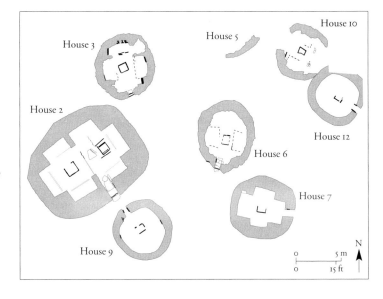

The Neolithic settlement of Barnhouse, Orkney: the house plans (especially 2 and 7) recall the cruciform plan of the Maes Howe burial chamber, while the square central hearth is reminiscent of the Stones of Stenness.

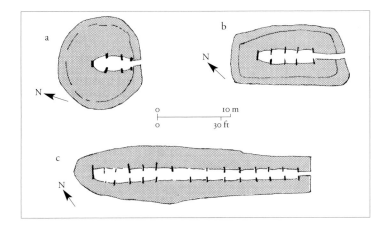

some 70 surviving or recorded sites, and have been divided into several different types. The most important distinction separates the Maes Howe-type tombs on the one hand from the so-called Orkney-Cromarty type on the other. The Maes Howe tombs are characterized by rectangular chambers entered via long narrow passages, and frequently have side cells or side chambers opening from the main chamber. They provide the most spectacular examples of Orkney Neolithic architecture, with tall corbelled vaults rising 5 m (16 ft) or more above the chamber floor. Orkney-Cromarty tombs form a less homogeneous category, and are much more numerous. They are also probably earlier in date than the Maes Howe tombs. The two main types of Orkney-Cromarty cairn are the tripartite cairn, with a chamber divided into three separate segments by pairs of vertical slabs projecting from the side walls, and the stalled cairn, in which the chamber is longer and the regularly spaced pairs of side-slabs create up to 14 separate compartments. Features shared by tripartite and stalled cairns are the relatively short passage and the linearity of the chamber. The final Orkney-Cromarty tomb type, the Bookan cairn, has a longer and narrower passage, with vertical slabs once again defining separate compartments. Their most curious feature, however, is their occasional semi-subterranean nature. The Bookan cairns of Taversoe Tuick and Huntersquoy are indeed two-storey structures, with upper and lower levels accessed by separate passages.

Neolithic chambered tombs of 'Maes Howe' type on Orkney: (a) Quanterness; (b) Wideford Hill; (c) Maes Howe.

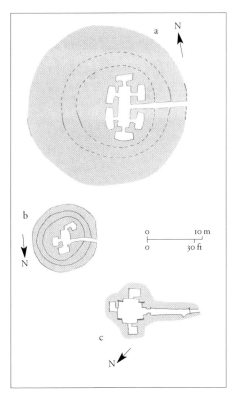

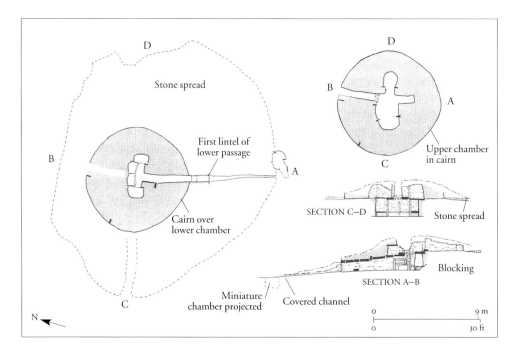

SECTION C–D

SECTION A–B

N

0   9 m

0   30 ft

Two-storey chambered tomb of Taversoe Tuick, Rousay, Orkney.

We have already noted the parallels between the plan of Maes Howe and the houses in the neighbouring settlement of Barnhouse. A still better-preserved settlement survives at Skara Brae on the western coast of the main island of Orkney. Here, eroding out of a cliff, was found a tightly built cluster of some half-dozen dry-stone houses, each with a single rectangular main room within a circular outer shell. In this relatively tree-less environment furniture was of stone, and beds and cupboards were built in. The nature of the construction strongly recalls that of Orkney chambered tombs, and the centralized cruciform plan, with entrance passage, beds and dresser, is especially close to that of some of the Maes Howe-type tombs. The radiocarbon dates from Skara Brae suggest that it was occupied for a period of several centuries between 3100 and 2500 BC; dates from tombs of Maes Howe type fall within the same Later Neolithic period.

This centralized design of Maes Howe-type tombs contrasts strongly with the linearity of the stalled and tripartite cairns. These, in turn, have domestic parallels in the Neolithic houses at Knap of Howar on the island of Papa Westray. This was a farmstead (rather than a village), consisting of two buildings immediately adjacent to each other and linked by interconnecting side doors. The main entrance from the outside was at the southern end of each building, where a short passage led through the thickness of the dry-stone wall. The interiors were divided up by cross-slabs into successive spaces, in a manner strikingly reminiscent of the stalled and tripartite cairns.

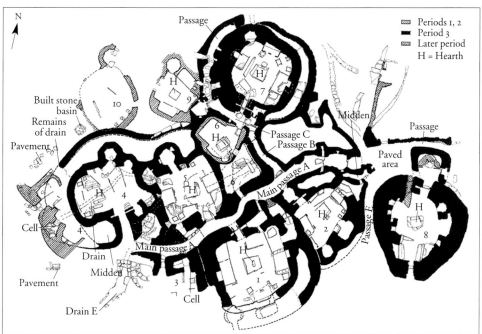

Top *Neolithic dry-stone houses of Skara Brae, Orkney.* Above *Plan of the Neolithic settlement of Skara Brae as revealed by the original excavations in the 1920s.*

Above *The Neolithic houses of Knap of Howar, Papa Westray, Orkney.*
Below *Interior of House no. 1 at Skara Brae: to the left is a bed and on the right, a 'dresser'; in the foreground is the central hearth.*

Radiocarbon dates from Knap of Howar place this farmstead around 3700 BC, in the Earlier Neolithic period. Thus both tombs and houses seem to show a transition from linearity in the Earlier Neolithic to centrality in the Later Neolithic, though not all tombs of Maes Howe type have such centralized plans as Maes Howe itself.

Manipulating the dead

The distinction between earlier and later Orkney tomb types involves more than simply tomb design; there is also a significant change in burial practices. The stalled cairn of Midhowe on Rousay may serve to illustrate the earlier phase. This is one of the longest stalled cairns, with side slabs dividing the interior into 24 separate compartments. A number of the compartments were equipped with stone benches or shelves that provided raised level surfaces on which the dead could be placed. Nine complete individuals had been laid out on these benches in crouched or sitting position, facing towards the interior of the tomb. There were also disarticulated remains both on the benches and on the ground beneath them, and in one case a complete body had been laid on the ground, even though the bench above it was unoccupied. Other individuals were represented only by their skulls. It appears from the variable completeness of the skeletons that bodies were whole when they were first brought into the tomb, but were displaced and became disarticulated as subsequent bodies were introduced. In one case, for example, the disarticulated bones had been gathered into a pile and the skull placed on top.

Midhowe is one of a group of stalled cairns on the southern side of Rousay. At another of them, Knowe of Yarso, there were disarticulated remains of several individuals in the passage and the outer compartments of the stalled cairn, but the inner zone was dominated by skulls: 17 in the end-compartment and 5 more in an adjacent side-compartment, all carefully

The Neolithic chambered tomb of Midhowe on Rousay, Orkney; it belongs to the 'stalled cairn' type, with a long chamber divided into compartments by pairs of vertical slabs.

The organization of funerary deposits in the stalled cairn of Midhowe (above) and Knowe of Yarso (below).

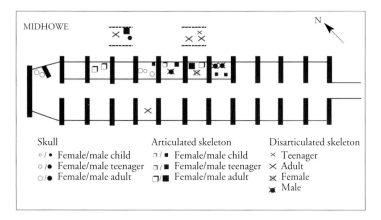

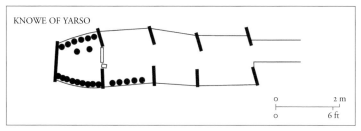

lined up along the wall of the tomb. The absence of mandibles (jaw bones) shows that these skulls were probably already defleshed when they were placed in position. There are more skulls than can be accounted for by the other skeletal elements, and it is possible that the

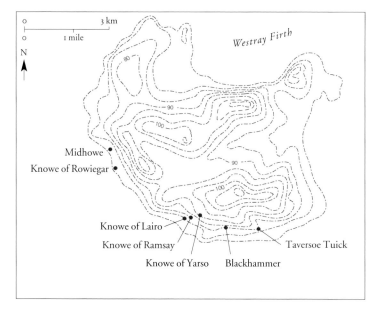

Map showing the location of Neolithic chambered tombs on the southern side of the island of Rousay, Orkney.

skulls were brought to Yarso from elsewhere. Perhaps the stalled cairns of Rousay were not intended to function individually, in isolation, but worked together as a kind of dispersed cemetery. The tombs on the lowest terrace, close to the sea's edge (Midhowe and Rowiegar), contain the largest proportion of articulated bodies. Those a little further upslope (Blackhammer and Ramsay) contain disarticulated skeletons, while those towards the top of the slope, such as Yarso, have a predominance of skulls, perhaps brought there from the nearby lower-lying tombs as the bodies decayed. Selected remains of the dead may thus have been passed from tomb to tomb as the bodies decayed, with the skulls singled out for special veneration and carefully placed in rows within the tombs that stood highest in the landscape.

These practices contrast with those documented for the later passage graves of Maes Howe type. In the first place, the numbers of individuals in the later tombs appear to be much greater. At Quanterness, excavation of part of the main chamber and one of the six side chambers recovered the remains of 157 individuals. From this it was estimated that the tomb as a whole must have contained almost 400 individuals. The remains were disarticulated, save for a small number of bodies placed in cists on the floor of the chamber, perhaps as foundation burials. The thick layer of disarticulated bone lying above them was initially thought to be the result of excarnation: the exposure of the bodies in the open air until the flesh had decayed. The argument was based on the observation that many of the bones were bleached, as if by exposure; but the presence of smaller hand and foot bones in the tomb suggested that excarnation is unlikely, since such bones are normally lost. We may envisage instead that the Quanterness bodies were brought into the tomb complete, but that the successive introduction of new bodies, over a use-life of perhaps several centuries. will have disturbed the earlier burials, leaving eventually a disturbed mass of disarticulated human bones.

The tomb of Isbister on South Ronaldsay provides further information on Orkney Neolithic burial practices. This belongs in architectural terms to the Orkney-Cromarty group, though its ground plan is anomalous and its burial evidence resembles rather the practices at tombs of Maes Howe type. The human remains at Isbister were from an estimated 341 individuals, though most were

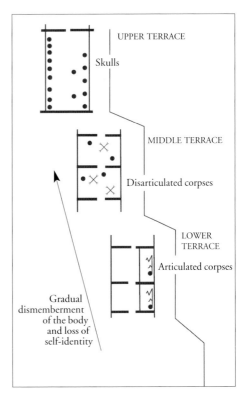

A recent model envisaging complementary roles for the Neolithic chambered tombs of Rousay.

UPPER TERRACE

Skulls

MIDDLE TERRACE

Disarticulated corpses

LOWER TERRACE

Articulated corpses

Gradual dismemberment of the body and loss of self-identity

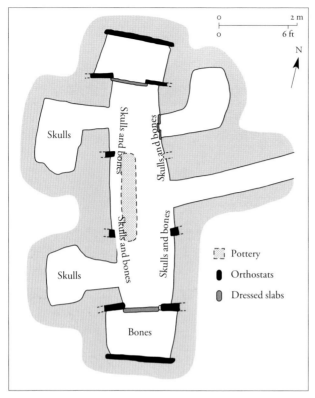

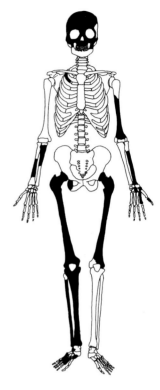

Above *Isbister, South Ronaldsay, Orkney: plan of the chamber showing the content and location of human bone deposits.*

Above right *The preserved elements (in black) of a single individual found in the tomb at Isbister – a woman aged around 35, found distributed between two separate sections of the main chamber (ST3 and ST4).*

represented by only fragments of the entire skeleton. Here again, therefore, other elements must have been removed for disposal elsewhere. Bones may indeed have been passed between tombs or among communities of the living. What is remarkable about Isbister is the evidence for the manner in which the human remains were sorted and selected between different parts of the tomb: skulls and long bones had been placed in groups along the rear wall of the main chamber; the end-cells with their mid-height shelves contained a mass of disarticulated remains; while the side-cells contained almost exclusively skulls.

At Isbister as at Quanterness it has been suggested that the bones had been brought into the tomb only after the bodies had been exposed and allowed to decompose outside; but this is a less likely explanation than that bodies were complete when brought into the tomb, and were broken up after they decayed. It was at this stage, too, that individual elements of the skeleton were selected and placed in different areas. The effect of such practices would have been to erase individual identity, but may also have marked a 'rite of passage' from the recently dead, decaying corpse to the clean, stabilized skeleton.

Prehistoric politics

The number and exceptional preservation of chambered tombs on the Orkney islands, and the variation in their size and morphology, has encouraged attempts to reconstruct the social and political structure of Neolithic Orkney. One early approach was to consider, as on Arran, that each tomb was built to serve an individual community. The distribution of tombs should therefore reflect the distribution of these small farming communities, even though there was little or no

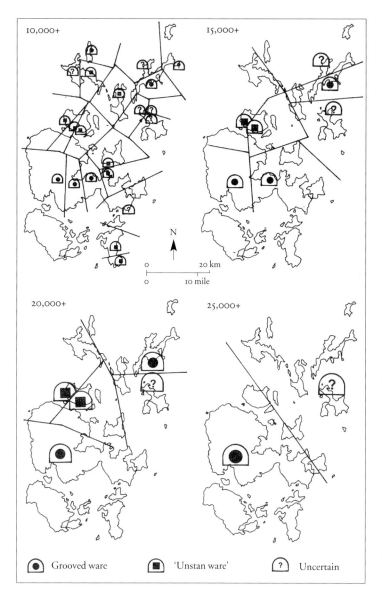

Political power in the Neolithic? An attempt to reconstruct the Neolithic sequence with a proposed division between two groups ('Grooved Ware' and 'Unstan Ware') and a progressively more hierarchical structure marked by the increasing investment of labour power in the construction of tombs; beginning in the first phase with numerous small structures each demanding c. 10,000 working hours to build; and culminating in a final stage of clustering into two large territories, each with its central tomb demanding over 25,000 working hours to build. This proposal for the centralization of power in Orkney during the Neolithic remains provocative, though looser and more egalitarian social structures are preferred by most archaeologists who study this material today.

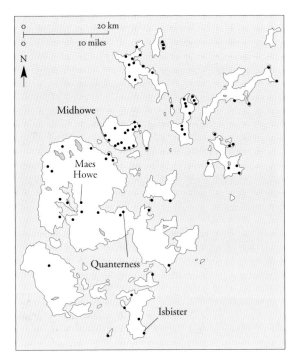

Distribution of Neolithic chambered tombs in Orkney.

evidence for the settlements themselves. Applied to the island of Rousay, this approach suggested the presence of a series of distinct 'territories' around the edges of the island, each with its tomb next to a small patch of arable land. The weakness of such an interpretation is that the tombs vary in size and need not have been in use at the same time or in the same way. Nor need they have been associated with individual small communities since they could have been used by the entire population of the island as a kind of dispersed cemetery.

Another approach takes the size variation and the chronology of the tombs as the basis for a political prehistory. Estimates of the time that would have been required to construct the tombs suggests that the smaller examples may have demanded fewer than 10,000 work-hours, whereas the largest and most complex, such as Maes Howe, may be the result of as much as 40,000 work-hours. When the tombs of different sizes are plotted on a map of the Orkney islands it emerges that the smallest are fairly evenly and widely distributed, whereas the largest tombs are much rarer, notably Maes Howe on Orkney mainland. This pattern can be given a chronological dimension also: beginning with an earlier period with many small tombs evenly spread across the islands and leading, no doubt gradually, to a later period when power was concentrated in only one or two centres.

The construction of the stone circles at Stenness and Brodgar might be seen as part of this process. Both stand at the centre of Orkney mainland, close to Maes Howe. Their creation (the cutting of the rock-cut ditch and the transport and erection of the stones) could have required as many as 100,000 work-hours. These were, in fact, the most labour-demanding of all Orkney Neolithic monuments, and the tight geographical clustering of Stenness, Brodgar and Maes Howe strongly suggests that this area was a centre of considerable significance in later Neolithic Orkney. Whether that significance is to be understood in terms of political power, however, remains open to question. Attempts to reconstruct Neolithic political structure and political development have tended to view the evidence in terms of modern Western social and political structures. It is clear that the

Neolithic population of the Orkney islands must have always been fairly small, and is unlikely to have lent itself to the kinds of centralized political formation that have sometimes been proposed.

Before leaving Orkney we must emphasize how exceptional it is in relation to the rest of Britain and Ireland. In first place, the number of Neolithic monuments that have been preserved is very striking. One explanation may be that Orkney has experienced less pressure from the development of arable farming in recent centuries, with the result that fewer sites have been destroyed. That may provide part of the answer, but most other Scottish islands can show nothing comparable, although Orkney is blessed with better arable land than, for example, the Outer and Inner Hebrides.

There is a second important respect in which Orkney is exceptional: the presence of Neolithic houses. Here again we must ask whether Orkney preserves something which has been largely destroyed elsewhere in Britain. The absence of timber on Orkney (which has always lacked substantial trees) forced Neolithic communities to build their houses of stone and turf, and the durable nature of the construction must play a significant part in the survival of sites such as Skara Brae and Barnhouse. As we have seen, a small number of Neolithic timber houses have been found in mainland Scotland, and they are rather more abundant in Ireland, but it remains the case that large areas of Britain lack any evidence of substantial Neolithic domestic structures. Here again, Orkney may be exceptional not only in the degree of preservation, but in the very character of Neolithic settlement itself.

Caithness

Crossing back to the mainland, the adjacent region of Caithness, despite its relatively desolate landscape, has a series of interesting and impressive megalithic tombs. The evidence indicates that many of these reached their final form through a protracted process of modification and accretion. A group of three chambered cairns at the northern end of Loch Calder illustrates this well, since their diverse morphology masks broadly comparable sequences of internal development. The westernmost and simplest of the three is Tulloch of Assery B, a round cairn some 20 m (66 ft) across with a single passage grave set off-centre

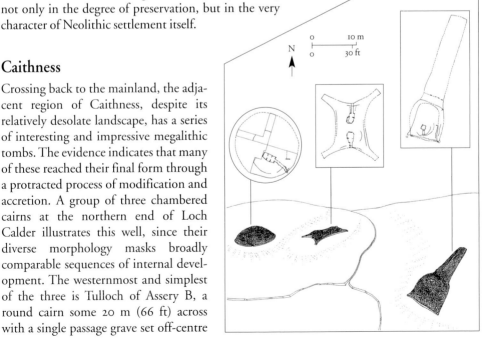

Neolithic monuments with complex cairns at Loch Calder, Caithness, at the northern extremity of Scotland: Tulloch of Assery B (left), Tulloch of Assery A, and (right) Tuloch an t'Sionnaich.

in its southeastern quadrant. The long passage leads to a rectangular chamber divided into three parts by pairs of projecting slabs. Its off-centre position indicates that this monument originated as a smaller circular cairn that was then enveloped within a larger circular monument extending to the north and west.

Tulloch of Assery A, a short distance to the east, is strikingly different in shape – a rectangular cairn with projecting horns at all four corners. In the centre of the concave northern and southern façades open matching passage graves, arranged back to back. It is likely that the southern passage grave is the earliest part of the monument and stood originally within its own small round cairn. Further east again, on the opposite side of a small stream, is Tulach an t'Sionnaich, a 60-m (196-ft) long cairn with a single chamber at its broader, southern end. Once again, the initial monument appears to have been a small circular cairn enclosing a passage grave. This was subsequently incorporated within a larger D-shaped cairn, with the straight edge forming a façade towards the south that completely blocked the passage entrance. The chamber must therefore have been taken out of

The long mound of Camster Long, Caithness, enclosing two passage graves.

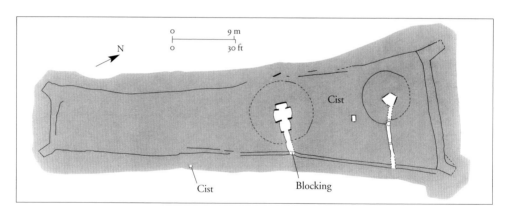

use by this enlargement. In the third and final phase, a long low tail was added to the north of this cairn.

Radiocarbon dates suggest that all three of the Loch Calder monuments were built and extended during the middle centuries of the 4th millennium BC. The contrasting plans were no doubt intentional, especially since, as we have seen, each of the three began as a small circular chambered cairn. The eventual counterpoint of the contrasting shapes may have been symbolically significant to the communities that built them, and illustrates an almost playful manipulation of the various cairn forms.

An analogous effect can be observed a few kilometres east of Loch Calder at Camster. Here an impressive 60-m (196-ft) long cairn stands along a prominent ridge, with a substantial round cairn on the lower ground to its south. Camster Long, like Tulloch of Assery A, has horned projections at all four corners, though the elongated form of the mound gives these a less striking appearance. The horns create a concave façade at either end of the cairn, but the passage graves do not open within these façades. Instead, the two passages lead from the long straight southern side of the cairn. Excavation has shown that each of the two passage graves was enclosed within its own circular cairn. These measured respectively 7.5 m and 9 m (25 ft and 30 ft) in diameter, and were originally free-standing structures. Only subsequently were the two circular cairns incorporated within the long cairn that we see today. Unlike Tulach an t'Sionnaich, however, the passages were not blocked when the long cairn was built; instead, they were extended to the edge of the mound, so that the chambers could still be accessed from outside. The only dating evidence for Camster Long came from an occupation surface beneath the tail of the long cairn, with pottery and flint and radiocarbon dates of 3900–3600 BC.

Camster Round, 19 m (62 ft) in diameter, has a tripartite chamber very similar to one of those in Camster Long, and the two tombs were probably contemporary. Recent experiments have shown that sounds produced within Camster Round (such as drumbeats) can be heard in

Camster Round, Caithness. The contrasting morphology of Camster Long (opposite) and Camster Round, located only 200 m (656 ft) apart, suggest an intentional counterpoint of different architectural forms on the part of the Neolithic builders.

Opposite *Camster Long, Caithness.*

the chambers of Camster Long, though it is difficult to establish whether this has any significance for the practices associated with these sites. The proximity of two mounds of contrasting morphology does suggest, however, as at Loch Calder, an intentional juxtaposition of different architectural forms, even though the chambers they contain are closely similar. The cairns of Caithness – horned, round or long – emerge from this analysis all the more clearly as visual statements placed in relation both to the landscape and to each other.

Balnuaran of Clava, Inverness: (above) distribution of Clava cairns; (below) plan of the cemetery of Balnuaran of Clava.

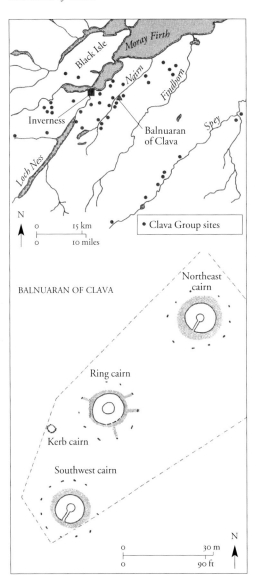

Clava Cairns and recumbent stone circles

In the area around Inverness in northeast Scotland there is a group of cairns that belong chronologically to the very final phase of chambered cairn construction in Scotland. Named Clava cairns after the site of Balnuaran of Clava, where a linear arrangement of such cairns lies along the floor of the Strathnairn valley, they for long proved difficult to date. Recent excavations, however, have shown that they belong to the Early Bronze Age. Radiocarbon dates from the northeast cairn at Clava fall between 2150 and 1700 BC, and are confirmed by results from other monuments of this class. These late dates are surprising, since the Clava cairns incorporate many of the features found in much earlier Scottish monuments, consisting of chambers built of orthostats standing within circular cairns edged by boulder kerbs. Some are passage graves, in the sense that a passage leads from the edge of the cairn into the central area; others are ring cairns, where the cairn forms an unbroken circle around a central space. Whether these chambers were ever roofed remains uncertain, though traces of corbelling have been observed and it is not impossible that they were covered by vaults in this way. The chambers are rather large, however, at approximately 4 m (13 ft) across, and the Clava cairns should perhaps be considered more akin to the recumbent stone circles described below.

Right *A cup-marked stone is incorporated in the kerb of the northeast cairn at Balnuaran of Clava.*

Below *Balnuaran of Clava: northeast cairn.*

Recent work at Clava has illustrated the careful choice of materials that their builders made. There is a particular interplay between the glacial erratics and the red sandstone blocks that had to be specially quarried from the nearby riverbank. The kerbs of the cairns show an irregular alternation of red and white stones, with black used only in the corbelling at the rear of the chambers. At dawn on the winter solstice, the sun's rays would have shone along the passages into the chambers of the two passage graves, illuminating the black stones built into the rear wall. It seems very probable that there was an intentional symbolism in the deployment of these differently coloured stones, related to the midwinter solstice.

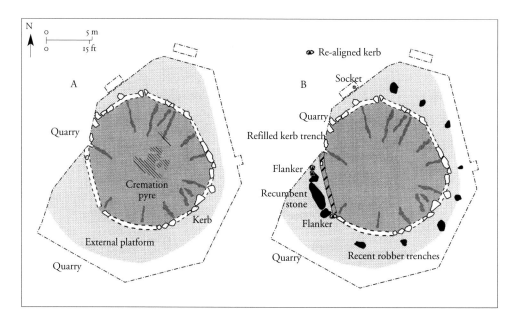

A

Quarry

Cremation
pyre

Kerb

External platform

Quarry

⚭ Re-aligned kerb

B   Socket

Quarry

Refilled kerb trench

Flanker

Recumbent
stone

Flanker

Quarry   Recent robber trenches

*Structural sequence at
Tomnaverie,
Aberdeenshire: a
cremation pyre
surrounded by a stone
kerb (left) was
subsequently transformed
into a recumbent stone
circle (right).*

Each of the three principal cairns at Balnuaran of Clava is encircled by a low stone platform. And beyond this is a ring of monoliths, a feature which ties these sites to the Scottish stone circle tradition. The most famous stone circles of northeast Scotland are the recumbent stone circles, in which the uprights are graded in height, the two tallest (known as 'flankers') framing a large stone laid on its side. This 'recumbent' stone has often been considered the focus of the circle, and usually lies in the southern sector of the ring. Often the recumbent is of a different geological material from the other stones of the circle, and contrasts with them in colour. Great care was also taken to ensure that the upper surface of the recumbent was as far as possible horizontal. Such careful design features have encouraged the search for astronomical alignments in the recumbent stone circles. The recumbent and flankers together clearly demarcate a portion of the horizon, providing in effect a kind of 'window'. The orientation of the recumbents lies outside the range of solar, lunar or significant stellar risings or settings, but may be directed towards the position of the midsummer full moon, which, to those positioned within the circle, would have appeared to pass over the recumbent.

Many recumbent stone circles have funerary cairns within them, and it was long believed that these were a later addition to the circles, which had originally been empty. Recent excavations at these sites, however, have shown that this sequence must be reversed. At Tomnaverie, the first stage saw the construction of a funeral pyre on a prominent hill. This was later enclosed (around 2600–2400 BC) within a rubble platform that was extended outwards and built up around its edges to counteract the natural hillslope. This platform or cairn was polygonal in shape and was structured internally by a series of radial walls; the whole was edged by a kerb of glacial erratics. In the final stage the recumbent stone circle was constructed – the sockets for the standing stones were cut down through the rubble supporting bank that had been laid around the outer edge of the stone platform. A similar sequence has been demonstrated at other sites. It thus seems that recumbent stone circles were not places at which celebrants or spectators could gather on summer nights to observe the full moon, but a special kind of funerary monument in which the cremation pyre

The recumbent stone circle of Loanhead of Daviot, Aberdeenshire.

The complex alignments of Upper Dounreay, Caithness: the four central groups of three or four parallel rows of small standing stones are flanked to north and south by less well-defined settings.

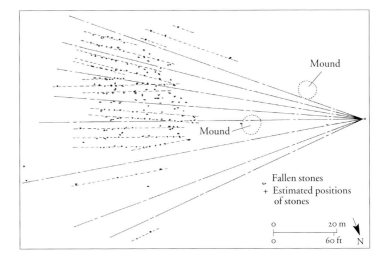

Mound

Mound

Fallen stones
+ Estimated positions of stones

0   20 m
0   60 ft   N

was encased in a cairn and enclosed within a ring. The recumbent stone itself, facing towards the midsummer moon, may therefore have been more for the benefit of the dead than for the living: a doorway modelled in stone, perhaps, but one that (as the excavator has said) had been shut.

Like the Clava cairns, or the wedge tombs of Ireland, the recumbent stone circles carry the megalithic tradition beyond the end of the Neolithic period into the late 3rd and early 2nd millennium BC. Other Scottish megalithic monuments may be later still. The fan-like multiple rows of standing stones at sites such as Mid-Clyth and Upper Dounreay in the far north belong probably to the Early or Middle Bronze Age. Like many elaborate settings of the kind, they have attracted astronomical explanations in recent decades, but are probably best to be seen as cumulative structures, added to and embellished by successive generations. And indeed the description 'megalithic' may here be misleading, as few of the many stones involved are more than 2 m (6.5 ft) tall.

CHAPTER THREE

England & Wales

THE NEOLITHIC MONUMENTS OF ENGLAND AND WALES, LIKE THOSE OF Scotland, include chambered and unchambered burial mounds, timber rings, earthwork enclosures and standing stones, these last sometimes arranged in rows or circles. The burial mounds are probably the earliest, the first of them dating to the early 4th millennium BC, within a few centuries of the introduction of pottery and domesticates that marks the beginning of the Neolithic. Portal dolmens, passage graves in small circular mounds, chambered long mounds, and 'unchambered' long mounds were all being built in different regions during the course of the 4th millennium. Towards the middle or end of the 4th millennium they were joined by cursus monuments and the round mounds which are a feature of northern England, and may find an echo in the oval mounds of southern England. Henges and the majority of the Neolithic stone circles follow in the 3rd

The portal dolmen of Pentre Ifan in southwest Wales.

millennium BC. Many structures, however, do not fit neatly into these traditional categories. The definition of 'henge', in particular, has posed problems, and some have urged that it be abandoned. Whether all these different monument types correspond to ideas or 'patterns' in the minds of the Neolithic builders remains open to question.

Portal dolmens and passage graves

In geographical terms a fundamental distinction can be drawn between Wales and western England on the one hand, where stone was widely available and monuments were often megalithic in construction, and the lowlands of the south and east on the other, where earth and timber predominated. In Wales and southwest England stone-built chambered tombs are most common, with three principal types: portal dolmens; passage graves in round mounds; and chambered long mounds of Cotswold-Severn type. In some areas, however, less formal chambers were created by the use of natural slabs and boulders. One such group are the 'outcrop sites' of southwest Wales, where a chamber was formed by levering up a natural slab to create a space beneath, underlining the link between tombs and the natural landscape. The megalithic tombs of Wales and southwestern England, with their striking use of unmodified natural blocks, may well have been inspired by the qualities of natural boulders and outcrops. It has even been suggested that some of these tombs were built on the sites from which their capstones were dug. Perhaps these stones were of special significance, long before the tomb was built, and what is true for the capstones may also apply to other elements of these structures. Built to contain burials, it can be conjectured that they also incorporated the power and symbolism of natural megalithic blocks.

This applies particularly to the portal dolmens of Cornwall and western Wales which are probably one of the earliest types of megalithic structure in southern Britain. Like the very similar monuments of Ireland (there usually known as 'portal tombs'), British portal dolmens take the form of a rectangular megalithic chamber dominated at one end by a portal formed by two tall

Distribution of the principal types of Neolithic funerary monument in Great Britain.

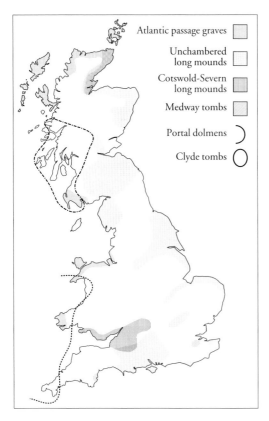

Atlantic passage graves

Unchambered long mounds

Cotswold-Severn long mounds

Medway tombs

Portal dolmens

Clyde tombs

1 Stones of Stenness: only four of the original 12 stones survive – they are considerably taller than those of the Ring of Brodgar. The angled tops recall the shapes of monoliths inside the Maes Howe chambered tomb nearby, and suggest that those too may originally have been part of a stone circle.

2 (Right) The Ring of Brodgar, the larger of the two stone circles on Orkney, with a rock-cut ditch 105 m (345 ft) in diameter enclosing 22 surviving stones, plus the stumps of several more. It is estimated that a total of around 60 may have formed the complete circle.

3 (Below left) Camster Long: one of the most impressive long cairns in Britain, on the crest of a low ridge in the remote moorland of northeast Scotland. The broader northeastern end of the cairn has a pair of low 'horns', but the passages leading to the two burial chambers open on to the longer, southeastern side of the cairn.

4 (Below right) The passage grave of Maes Howe stands at the centre of a circular bank and ditch which recalls contemporary henge monuments. Neolithic burial mounds within large circular enclosures are also known at Duggleby Howe in Yorkshire and Ballynahatty in Ireland.

5 (Above) Recent survey has revealed that the current conical shape of Silbury Hill is the product of centuries of erosion and that the mound was not a circular monument but a polyhedron with up to nine straight sides.

6 (Left) Waylands Smithy, with a façade of six megalithic sarsen pillars, the largest of them over 3 m (10 ft) in height, flanking the entrance to the burial chamber at the southern end of the long cairn. Excavation in 1919 recovered remains of 8 individuals within the chamber, but the majority of the burial deposit had already been removed.

7 (Above) Pentre Ifan, southwest Wales, is a classic portal
dolmen with a large sloping capstone elevated on thin
pillars. Excavations in the 1930s discovered the foundations
of an enclosing cairn, but it may have been no more than a
low platform around the foot of the uprights.

8 (Left) Carreg Samson, southwest Wales, consists of a
polygonal megalithic chamber roofed by a massive capstone,
supported on uprights of contrasting petrology. Symmetries
of this kind are unlikely to have arisen by chance and
illustrate the careful deployment of materials in building
these structures.

9 (Left) A pillar (replica of the original) decorated with serpentiform motifs, found covering a pit at the centre of the mound behind the chamber at Bryn Celli Ddu, Anglesey. The decorated stone may belong to a stone circle that preceded the passage grave on this site.

10 (Right) Barclodiad y Gawres, Anglesey, orthostat C16: two lozenges flanked by serpentiform motifs with zigzags and a spiral above. Unlike Bryn Celli Ddu (above) the decorated stone comes from the passage grave itself, and was positioned at the junction of passage and chamber.

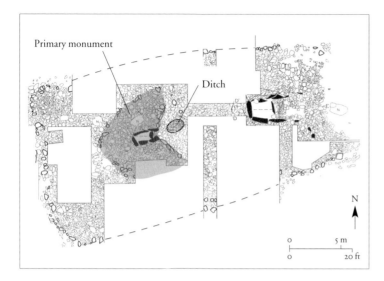

Primary monument

Ditch

N

o   5 m

o   20 ft

Plan of Dyffryn Ardudwy in northwest Wales: the primary monument (a portal dolmen) was subsequently incorporated within and sealed by an oblong cairn with a second megalithic chamber.

matching pillars with a blocking slab between them. The capstone rests on the portal stones and slopes downwards towards the rear of the chamber. Portal dolmens are also distinguished by the way the massive capstone is supported on often slender uprights, making it appear, as has recently been described, as if the capstone is 'floating'.

The question of whether or not portal dolmens were entirely hidden within their cairns has not been resolved, though their distinctive chamber form argues that they were designed to be visible. Perhaps the cairns were no more than low surrounding platforms. At Dyffryn Ardudwy in northwest Wales, a portal dolmen with its own small platform or cairn had been incorporated within a larger cairn that enclosed a second and larger megalithic chamber; in front of the western chamber, sealed by the enlarged cairn, was a pit containing Early Neolithic pottery. The early dating of portal dolmens as a whole rests largely on the pottery from this site.

Burial deposits are rare and seem mostly to be Bronze Age insertions and so provide little help in dating. This absence of Neolithic burial deposits may indeed lead us to question whether the portal dolmens should properly be described as tombs. The Pentre Ifan portal dolmen, with its dramatic inclined capstone, was built within a pit from which the capstone might have been dug. Thus, it has been suggested, the elevation and display – perhaps veneration – of a natural earth-fast boulder may have been the key intention. On the other hand, Irish portal tombs do contain human remains, and the Dyffryn Ardudwy portal dolmen in its cairn is clearly analogous to other types of megalithic tomb from western Britain. They may hence be tombs after all, though the prominence of the capstones suggests these were symbolically important.

Above *Passage grave of Trefignath, Anglesey.*

Below *Passage grave of Bryn Celli Ddu, Anglesey.*

Another early monument tradition in the west – perhaps as early as the portal dolmens – is that of passage graves. As we have seen, these are one of the commonest Neolithic monument types in western and northern Scotland, and they are also found in Wales and southwest England. They are clustered in areas facing the Irish Sea, with an extension eastwards into Wessex and a small group of outliers in Kent around the River Medway.

One specific type of passage grave that is restricted to Wales and southwestern England is the passage grave within a small circular mound or cairn. These appear to form a regionally distinct tradition which may have been linked to developments in Scotland, Ireland and perhaps northwest France. The earliest of these small passage graves have polygonal chambers and short passages: for example, the primary chamber of Trefignath on Anglesey, or Broadsands in Devon. They have been interpreted by some as evidence of a single diaspora, though it should be noted that burial practices within the group are variable (successive inhumation at Broadsands, cremation at other examples). A later group of passage graves is largely concentrated in northwest Wales, with close connections across the Irish Sea to the Boyne Valley tombs. The group includes Barclodiad y Gawres on Anglesey, which has megalithic art like the Boyne Valley tombs and yielded human remains that had been cremated, as is customary also in Irish megalithic tombs, but rare in Britain. Barclodiad y Gawres is one of only two or three decorated megalithic tombs in southern Britain, with five decorated stones.

Bryn Celli Ddu on Anglesey also belongs to this later group of passage graves, but is of additional interest in demonstrating how burial mounds may have been related to other types of Neolithic monument. Barcoldiad y Gawres on the same small island is a cruciform-plan passage grave with five decorated orthostats (large upright supporting stones) – two facing each other at the ends of the

Megalithic art in Wales: a decorated orthostat from the passage grave of Barclodiad y Gawres, Anglesey.

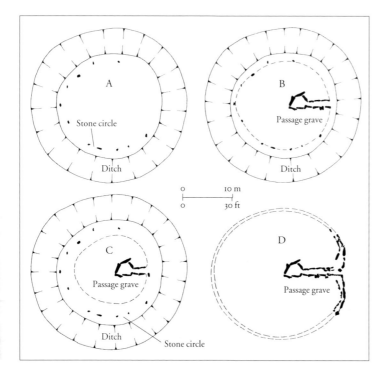

Alternative visions by different archaeologists of the structural sequence at Bryn Celli Ddu: A primary phase with stone circle enclosed within a ditch (Michael O'Kelly); B primary phase with passage grave covered by a small circular mound edged by a kerb of standing stones and enclosed within a ditch (George Eogan); C primary phase with passage grave covered by a small circular mound surrounded by a stone circle and a ditch (Richard Bradley). All agree on the final phase, D, when the tail of the mound covers the infilled ditch.

transepts, and two more framing the entrance into the chamber from the passage. Bryn Celli Ddu, on the other hand, had only a single decorated stone, hidden away in the heart of the mound, immediately behind the chamber. Furthermore, this stone was decorated on two opposite faces, suggesting that it had originally stood not as a kerbstone or orthostat, but as a free-standing monolith. Excavations in the 1930s revealed the sockets of a circle of standing stones that had stood within a ring-ditch that was later covered by the edges of the mound. This has been interpreted in various ways, but one possibility is that the passage grave was preceded by a small stone circle within a ditch, and that the decorated stone formed a part of this earlier structure. If so, then at Bryn Celli Ddu a stone circle was later transformed into a passage grave. The same transformation has been proposed at Maes Howe in Orkney, as we have seen, while in other cases, as at Newgrange in Ireland, the opposite process occurred, with a passage grave later encircled by a ring of standing stones. These instances serve to illustrate how different types of Neolithic monument might adjoin or succeed each other on the same site.

Chambered long mounds

Chambered long mounds or 'Cotswold-Severn' tombs are among the best known of British megalithic monuments, and have been the subject of systematic exploration and excavation since the early 19th century. The classic form is an elongated trapezoidal cairn with a concave façade at the broader end. In some cases the concavity is accentuated to the point where the centre of the façade is recessed between incurving horns. The chambers can be arranged either as a pair, opening from opposite long sides of the cairn, or as single axial

Cotswold-Severn long mounds, with chambers arranged either laterally (above) or axially (below). Note the axial 'false portal' at Belas Knap.

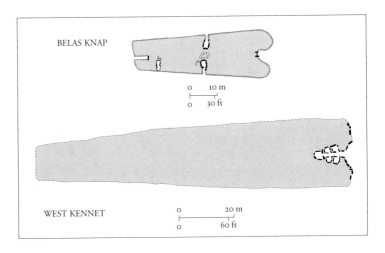

BELAS KNAP

0   10 m

0   30 ft

WEST KENNET

0   20 m

0   60 ft

chamber, opening from an entrance in the middle of the façade. The terminal chambers are usually of transepted plan (though simple terminal chambers are also known). Even where the chambers are placed in the sides of the mound, however, the façade played an important symbolic function. This can be seen for example at Belas Knap, Gloucestershire, where the centre of the recessed façade is occupied by a false portal consisting of two uprights and a lintel, with a flat slab where the opening would be. The entrances to the burial chambers,

Above The Cotswold-Severn long mound of Belas Knap.

Left The 'false door' located in an axial position between the horns of the long mound at Belas Knap.

by contrast, are in the sides of the mound. We may conjecture that the 'false portal' at Belas Knap, as at other sites, was intended to permit people gathered in the forecourt to communicate with the dead, or to allow the spirits of the dead to enter and leave the tomb.

The transepted passage graves of Cotswold-Severn tombs, such as Wayland's Smithy (Oxfordshire), Nympsfield (Gloucestershire) and West Kennet (Wiltshire), are the most elaborate megalithic chambers in England and Wales. They were used for collective inhumations, with skeletal elements from several dozen individuals mixed together in the burial spaces. At West Kennet, the human remains in the various cells of the transepted chamber gave evidence of differences in the treatment the dead. Thus the terminal cell, excavated by John Thurnam in 1859, contained crouched inhumations of five adult males and a child, whereas the southeast and southwest cells, excavated by Stuart Piggott around a century later in 1955–56, contained mainly juveniles and elderly respectively. A degree of lateral symmetry was also observed, in that the human remains in the southern cells were more disarticulated than those in the northern cells. Furthermore, the bodies of adult males appear to have been less likely to undergo rigorous disarticulation than those of women or juveniles. Thus different categories of the dead were treated in different ways, and the subdivisions of the transepted chamber were probably used to structure these differences.

Cotswold-Severn tombs may have been built within a relatively restricted time-interval and some had a relatively short use-life. At Hazleton North (Gloucestershire), the northern and southern chambers may have remained in use for little more than a century (3780–3640 BC). Careful study of the remains at Hazleton has also documented the way in which the dead were interred. It seems that bodies were brought intact into the chamber, but then pushed to the side when further corpses were introduced. Some elements, notably long bones and skulls, had subsequently been removed. The result was a mass of largely disarticulated human bones, with parts of individual bodies scattered widely between passage and chamber. One chance event provides a snapshot of the process: an orthostat in the northern inner passage collapsed during the use of the tomb, blocking access to the chamber.

Subsequent interments in this northern passage grave were therefore restricted to the outer passage. The last burial of all was a fully articulated body laid at the very end of the outer passage, called the 'flintknapper' from the material associated with him. Other Cotswold-Severn tombs, however, may have witnessed different practices. At Parc le Breos Cwm in South Wales, the disarticulated remains in the chamber were more fragmented and weathered than those in the passage, and some bore marks of chewing by carnivores.

Above *The long mound of West Kennet near Avebury.*

Below *Isometric view of the eastern end of the West Kennet long mound, showing the megalithic façade and the transepted chamber.*

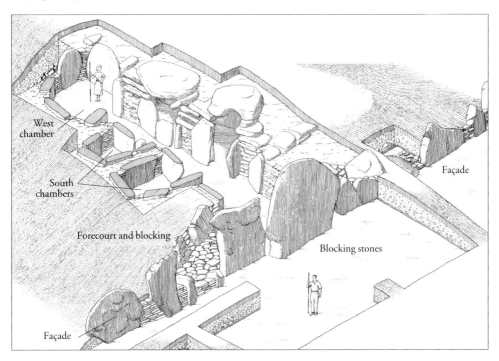

The 'flintknapper' skeleton as found in the outer part of the passage of the northern passage grave at Hazleton North, Gloucestershire.

Detail of the 'flintknapper' skeleton at Hazleton North.

It is possible that some at least of the bodies in this chamber had been exposed before they were brought into the tomb. Equally, as in the Orkney tombs described earlier, there is evidence that bones had been removed: this may account for the deficit of skulls and long bones at Hazleton North, and isolated human remains may well have circulated both between different parts of a tomb, between different chambers or between different tombs, and been taken to other kinds of site.

The standardized plans of Cotswold-Severn tombs should not obscure the fact that some are clearly multi-phase structures. A good example is Notgrove (Gloucestershire), where the first stage involved the construction of a small megalithic chamber with corbel-vaulted roof standing within a circular dry-stone rotunda. The rotunda measured some 7 m (23 ft) in diameter by 0.76 m (2.5 ft) high, and enclosed a polygonal cist, made from thin slabs of local limestone and containing the remains of a single adult inhumation. In a subsequent stage this circular monument was sealed within a classic Cotswold-Severn cairn. Whether the Notgrove rotunda was ever intended to be a free-standing structure, however, is unclear. A similar structure within the Ty Isaf cairn (southeast Wales) was apparently bonded-in with the Cotswold-Severn cairn around it, suggesting that both were part of the same building project. However tempting it is to interpret these circular rotundas as primary monuments, only later incorporated within Cotswold-Severn cairns, the case has yet to be proved; they may simply be part of the building process. And it is clear that other Cotswold-Severn tombs were built in a single straightforward sequence, as shown for instance by the regular cellular construction at Hazleton North.

Ty Isaf, southeast Wales: a Cotswold-Severn long mound with lateral chambers apparently built on to a circular cairn, also enclosing a passage grave.

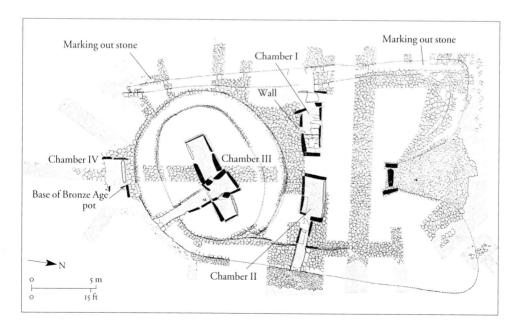

Marking out stone

Marking out stone

Chamber I

Wall

Chamber IV

Chamber III

Base of Bronze Age pot

N

Chamber II

o   5 m

o   15 ft

Artist's reconstruction of the primary phase of the Street House monument, North Yorkshire.

Opposite above
Timber structures of the chamber at Haddenham during excavation.

Opposite below
Haddenham, Cambridgeshire: the bedding trenches (left) and preserved timber structures (right) of the façade and chamber of the long mound.

Unchambered long mounds

In eastern England and eastern Scotland, long mounds of earth or chalk without any megalithic or stone-built chamber were raised during the 4th millennium BC. They may have been built over a period of a millennium or more, though many of them have been dated to the centuries around 3800–3600 BC. Some cover the remains of a timber mortuary structure that was burned before the mound was built. In these cases, the human remains are confined to the destroyed mortuary structure, and so the mound could be interpreted simply as a marker, covering that particular location. In other cases, as for example at the three Avebury barrows of Horslip, South Street and Beckhampton Road in Wiltshire, no trace of any mortuary structure was found, nor any human remains. A better interpretation may therefore be to dissociate the mound from the underlying mortuary structure. This can be illustrated by the site of Street House in North Yorkshire, where the structures revealed by excavation resembled ones that might have been expected before a covering mound was built. A curving timber façade had at its centre a massive timber post which blocked one end of a narrow timber mortuary house, 1 m (3 ft) wide and 7.2 m (24 ft) long, ending at another massive post-hole. The mortuary house probably had a raised timber floor, with wooden rafters to support a brushwood or turf roof, weighted down by sandstone blocks. The whole structure was eventually burned down, along with the façade, as an intentional act.

Timber mortuary structures similar to that at Street House have been discovered beneath many long mounds in eastern England, and perhaps the only difference is that whoever burned down the Street House mortuary structure decided not to build a mound over the remains. The timber chambers at Haddenham, Fussell's Lodge (Wiltshire) and Wayland's Smithy were also long and narrow, and though some of these mortuary structures were fronted by a forecourt or antechamber, there appears to have been no intention of providing permanent access. Most were burned before the mound was built over them. We must conclude that these are not timber versions of passage graves, but a specific form of monument that has no close analogue in stone.

The best-preserved Neolithic timber mortuary structure was excavated in the waterlogged Fenland at Haddenham, 15 km (9 miles) north of Cambridge, in 1986. The chamber was built of large slabs of wood up to 4 m (13 ft) long and 10 cm (4 in) thick, that is similar in size to the

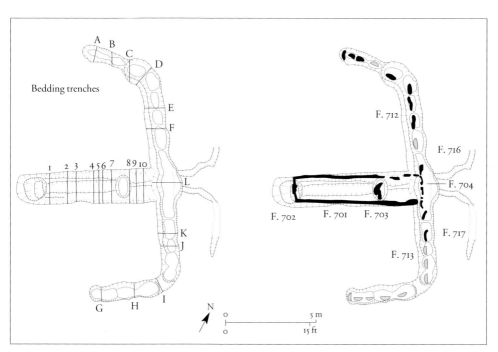

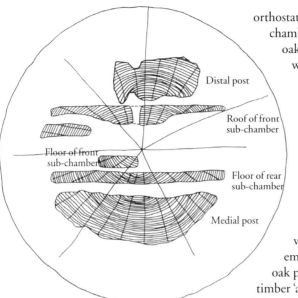

Distal post

Roof of front
sub-chamber

Floor of front
sub-chamber

Floor of rear
sub-chamber

Medial post

Above *Diagram
showing the derivation of
the timber elements from
the Haddenham chamber
from a single massive oak
tree trunk.*

orthostats of a megalithic tomb. Most of the chamber elements were taken from a single oak trunk, some 300–400 years old, which had been split not radially, following the grain, but transversely. A particularly massive element was the medial post, a split oak trunk 1.5 m (5 ft) across, that divided the mortuary structure into chamber and forecourt. The mortuary structure was supported by a wide earth bank built up around it, and access can only have been possible through the narrow opening at the east end, or via the roof. The opening at the east emerged in the centre of a façade of split oak posts, with a more slightly built pair of timber 'antennae' walls projecting in front of it and forming a funnel-shaped approach to the chamber entrance. At the end of its use, the chamber was carefully dismantled and burned; it was probably only after that stage that a long mound was built over the remains.

At Haddenham, bones of only five partially disarticulated individuals were found at the rear of the chamber, but many of these timber mortuary houses have much larger skeletal deposits. At Fussell's Lodge, remains of between 53 and 57 individuals were recovered from

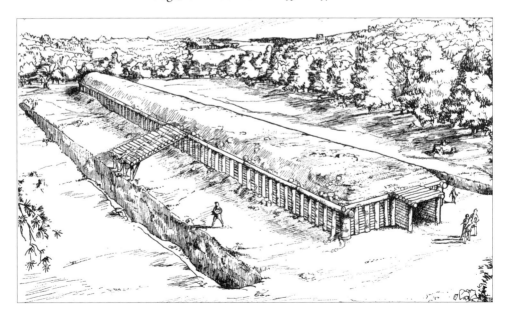

the remains of the timber mortuary house, but these were mostly represented by considerably less than the normal skeletal complement. The discovery of human skeletal elements in pits and ditches, and notably in the contemporary causewayed enclosures (see p. 102) where they are a regular feature, suggests that once disarticulated, fragments of bodies may have circulated as relics in Neolithic Britain, ultimately coming to rest in a variety of locations. Thus human remains were far from restricted to so-called burial mounds, and their presence within mortuary houses and megalithic chambers forms part of a more general distribution of human remains among Neolithic sites of diverse types.

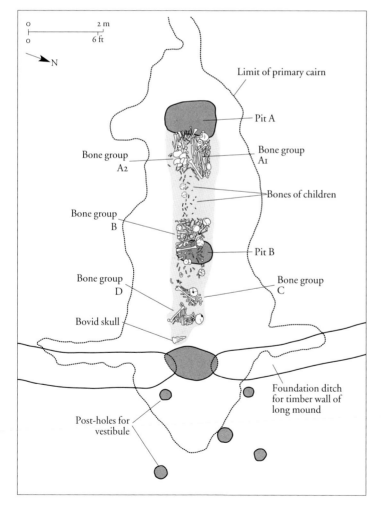

Plan of the mortuary house of Fussell's Lodge with three substantial post-holes (pits A, B & C) and separate deposits of human bone (bone groups A1, A2, B and C).

Opposite below Fussell's Lodge, Hampshire: a reconstruction of the long mound with flanking ditches and external timber wall supported by posts.

Later Neolithic burials

The 'classic' burial monument of the British Neolithic is the chambered tomb or mortuary house containing multiple and often disarticulated inhumations. During the 3rd millennium BC, however, an alternative tradition developed which was to continue into the Bronze Age: the practice of individual burial under a round or oval mound. The origins of this tradition lie in the 4th millennium BC: three graves with single articulated individuals are known at Radley in the Thames Valley, and another at Windmill Hill in Wiltshire. There was also an oval barrow with a double burial, and a mortuary pit with three articulated and partially articulated burials. In southern Britain, alongside the more numerous long mounds, a number of oval mounds are dated to the period 3700–2800 BC. Such oval mounds may merely be shorter versions of the earlier mounds, though in the case of long mounds the dead were always buried in above-ground structures, either stone chambers or timber mortuary houses, rather than pits cut into the ground surface.

In northeastern England the custom appears to have been for round, rather than oval mounds, and some cover multiple inhumations. At Callis Wold in East Yorkshire, the mound overlay a rectangular stone platform, with a substantial timber post at either end, on which had been placed 10 contracted adult bodies. Further disarticulated remains (including the skull and long bones of an infant) were recovered from the fill of the two post-holes. A low tumulus was first heaped over this arrangement, followed by a larger two-stage round mound, probably all within the middle centuries of the 4th millennium BC. The largest and most famous of the Neolithic round mounds is, however, Duggleby Howe, some 16 km (10 miles) further north. The central feature here is a shaft grave 2.7 m (9 ft) deep cut into the chalk bedrock, with a shallower grave to its east, both covered by a primary mound 23 m (75 ft) in diameter and 3.4 m (11 ft) high. The shaft grave contained no fewer than seven individual inhumations at different levels within its fill, and in the adjacent, shal-

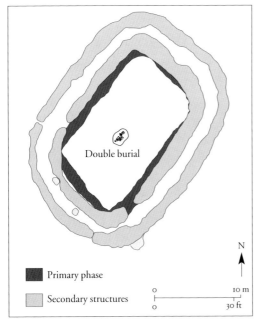

Double burial

Primary phase

Secondary structures

0   10 m

0   30 ft

N

Left Radley: central pit with double burial enclosed by a double ditch defining a sub-rectangular area indicating the location of an oval mound.

lower grave there was a sequence of three more. Several of these burials were accompanied by grave goods, and two of them in particular (inhumations C and G) were interpreted as 'prestige' burials. In addition to the inhumations, there were 53 cremations within the mound, mainly in its upper part, perhaps representing a shift to cremation from inhumation during the 3rd millennium BC. In a final phase the Duggleby Howe mound was enlarged to a height of 6.5 m (21 ft) by just under 40 m (131 ft) across. At some stage, perhaps before this, it was encircled by an incomplete bank and ditch forming a huge enclosure 370 m (1215 ft) in diameter, an arrangement reminiscent of Maes Howe in Orkney.

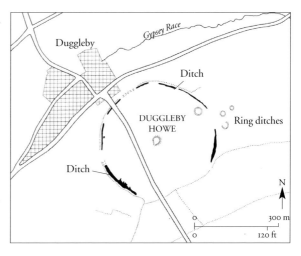

These Neolithic round mounds prefigure the much more numerous round mounds with single graves that are associated with Beaker pottery and the Early Bronze Age. They indicate a significant change in attitudes towards the dead compared with the earlier Neolithic chambered tombs. No longer was prolonged access to the dead required or desired. Indeed, many chambered tombs may have been blocked at just this period, preventing further access. The growing frequency of cremation burial (though still a minority practice) underlines the same point: the dead were now being consigned to eternity in a definitive way, without provision for future interventions in the grave for the removal of body parts or the insertion of new corpses. The new practices removed the bodies of the dead from the presence of the living. At the same time, they provided the opportunity for a greater emphasis on the status of the

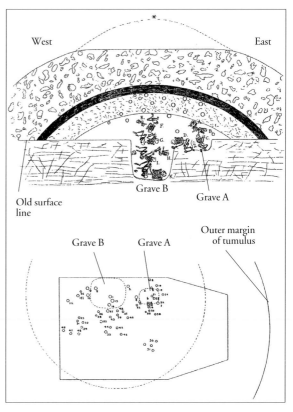

individual. Funerary ceremonies at single graves may have been performances carried out in full view of the assembled community, at which the treatment given to the dead body, and the objects placed with it in the grave, signified both the importance of the deceased and the social relationships among the living. It is hence not surprising that it was in this context, at the very end of the Neolithic period, that richly furnished graves first make their appearance.

Henges and cursus monuments

The circular enclosure around the 'Great Barrow' at Duggleby Howe may be a precursor of the henge monuments that appear in many parts of England during the 3rd millennium BC. Along with stone and timber circles, cursus monuments and pit circles, henges belong to a varied category of British Neolithic monuments that were not exclusively associated with burial but may have been intended for ceremonial gatherings and processions.

The name 'henge' is perhaps unfortunate, being derived from Stonehenge, which in a number of respects is far from typical of this type of monument. For a start, the classic henge does not necessarily contain stone structures, but consists simply of a circular ditch with an external bank. And at Stonehenge, the bank lies on the inside edge of the ditch, which again makes it unusual. The fact that in most henges the bank lies outside the ditch refutes any suggestion that they may have been defensive in function. The henge banks instead will have served to enhance the sense of an enclosed sacred space, an area set apart from everyday activity, hiding ceremonies within the enclosure from external scrutiny. They provide in fact a kind of enclosed arena.

Henges are rather variable in size and shape, from small examples less than 20 m (66 ft) across to the massive Wiltshire enclosures of Durrington Walls and Avebury, over 200 m (656 ft) in diameter. In their classic form they are often remarkably regular in appearance: strikingly circular in plan, with either a single entrance or two opposed entrances on the same axis. Other henges are less regular in plan, and some contain post-holes or stone settings within their interiors. Dating evidence places them in the Late Neolithic – the middle centuries of the 3rd millennium BC.

One of the most remarkable sets of henges is at Thornborough in Yorkshire (see pp. 90–91). Here a group of three henges – the largest outside Wessex – stand in line along a valley floor. Each measures 240 m (788 ft) in diameter and has an opposed pair of entrances oriented northwest/southeast. Each of them also has a second external ditch and bank, a feature which is found at three nearby Yorkshire henges, but is otherwise known only at Dorchester-on-Thames (p.

96). The northernmost of the Thornborough henges is the best preserved, with the inner bank still standing 3 m (10 ft) high and 18 m (60
ft) wide, separated from the inner ditch (itself 20 m/66 ft) across) by a
level space 12 m (40 ft) wide. These dimensions serve to illustrate the
scale of henge constructions, which may have been the work of
Neolithic communities coming together in these special sacred locations from a wide surrounding area.

The Thornborough henges were not the only nor the earliest
Neolithic monuments on the site. Running across the southern edge
of the central henge, and clearly pre-dating it, was a cursus monument, originally over 1.2 km (0.75 mile) long and 43 m (141 ft) wide.
The end of a second possible cursus at right angles to the first, appears
alongside the northern henge on aerial photographs. Cursus monuments were first named as such in the 18th century, when Stukeley
suggested that the long linear enclosure below Stonehenge may have
been a race course (Latin 'cursus') in Neolithic times. Today they are
more often interpreted as processional ways, though there is little firm
evidence for their use. They frequently occur in association with other
monuments, as at Thornborough. Over 50 are known in England,
with a further 50 in Scotland and Wales and some half a dozen examples recently identified in Ireland, including at Tara and Newgrange.

Cursus monuments are defined by parallel banks with external
ditches, typically enclosing a corridor around 50 m (164 ft) in width,
closed off at either end. They vary considerably in length, the longest
of all being the Dorset cursus in southwest England, which has a total
length of 9.8 km (6 miles), though it may be viewed as two separate
monuments end to end. It incorporates a long mound in its earthwork banks, which indicates both the continuity of this ritual

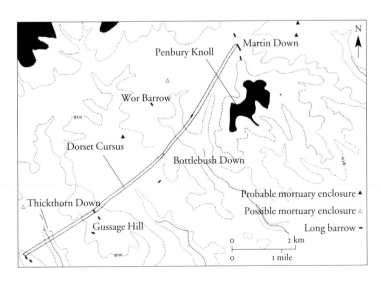

*Plan of the Dorset Cursus
showing other Neolithic
monuments incorporated
into its banks or located
nearby.*

landscape and the fact that the cursus is later than the long mounds. Radiocarbon dates suggest indeed that cursus monuments were built during the middle or later part of the 4th millennium BC. They are closely associated with a second class of linear monument, the 'bank barrow', first identified at Maiden Castle in Dorset, where within the Iron Age hillfort a linear bank 540 m (1772 ft) long flanked by ditches on either side was excavated in the 1930s. The close connection between bank barrows and cursus monuments is emphasized by hybrid monuments such as the Cleaven Dyke in Scotland, described earlier (pp. 25–26), which combine elements of both. Their extraordinary dimensions, stretching often for several kilometres across the landscape, would have made them among the most impressive of all

Opposite Thornborough Neolithic complex: an aerial photograph taken in 1945 before gravel quarrying. In the foreground is the southern henge; the wooded area in the background marks the position of the northern henge.

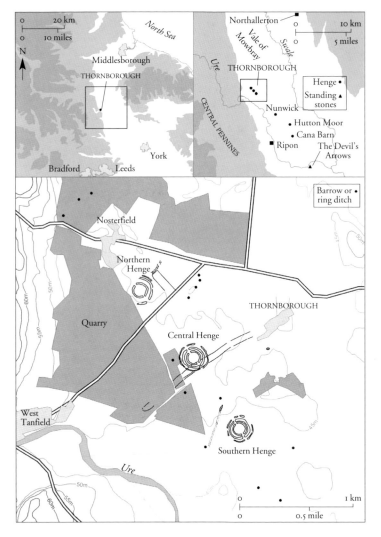

Maps showing the position of Thornborough, and a plan of the Neolithic complex.

British Neolithic monuments, carving up the terrain and obstructing movement.

The dating evidence indicates that henges and cursus monuments belong to different periods of the British Neolithic. Cursus monuments, along with chambered tombs, unchambered long mounds and causewayed enclosures (see p. 102), are characteristic of the earlier Neolithic; henges, together with stone circles, fall within the later Neolithic. It has recently been suggested that this could correspond to a change in religious beliefs or practices during the late 4th or early 3rd millennium BC. Circular enclosures, such as Stonehenge, or those around burial mounds at Maes Howe in Orkney, Duggleby Howe in Yorkshire, and Newgrange, Tara and Ballynahatty in Ireland, may represent the first stage in this transition, during the early 3rd millennium BC. They were followed, in Britain at least, by classic henges, which appeared around 2800 BC and continued to be built and used as centres of ceremonial activity for 500 years, up to the end of the Neolithic period.

Stone and timber circles

Closely related to the henges are the stone and timber circles of England and Wales. As in Scotland and Ireland, geology plays a major part in their distribution: stone circles are found mainly in southwest Britain and Cumbria, regions where stone was readily available. At a general level, the distribution of stone circles complements that of the henges we have just discussed: stone circles are found mainly in the western upland regions, the henges in eastern lowland areas where stone was hard to come by. This cannot be the whole explanation, however. In the first place, we must distinguish between those henges with entirely open interiors, and those with circular timber circles. Timber circles are sometimes enclosed within henge-type circular embankments. Stone circles also sometimes stand within structures that might otherwise be described as henges, though it appears that in these cases the stone settings were generally a later addition.

Yet the classic henges of eastern and southern Britain are not simply stone-less versions of stone circles. To begin with, there is a systematic difference in locations. Stone circles are generally placed in upland settings with broad views across the landscape. In terms of visibility they are essentially permeable: a person inside them can see the surrounding terrain; while a person outside can see into the interior, since the stones themselves only partially block the view. Henges, on the other hand, are generally located on valley floors, where long-range vistas are not available. The effect of enclosure is enhanced by the high banks, which, as we have already remarked, serve to conceal activities within the henge from outside observers, and hide the adjacent landscape from people inside the henge. Stone circles are also generally much smaller than henges. Henges and stone circles are therefore not simply highland and lowland variants of the same essential structure, differentiated merely by the choice of materials; they are monuments of fundamentally different form and function.

Some of the largest, and possibly the earliest, stone circles in England and Wales are found in Cumbria, an area of mountains and lakes that is also notable for the quarrying and production of polished stone axes of Great Langdale tuff. The first of the Cumbrian circles, such as Castlerigg, Long Meg and her Daughters and Swinside, may have been constructed around 3000 BC or even a little earlier. One of the most impressive is Castlerigg, a setting of 38 stones forming a circle 33 m (108 ft) across, with a clearly marked entrance on the northern side flanked by a pair of taller stones. Further south, a second group of stone circles is found in Peak District of Derbyshire. Once again this is an upland area where stone is abundant. Probably the most famous Peak District stone circle is Arbor Low, where a ring of fallen stones stands within a henge-type monument: a circular bank some 75 m (246 ft) across with internal ditch and opposed

The stone circle of Castlerigg in Cumbria.

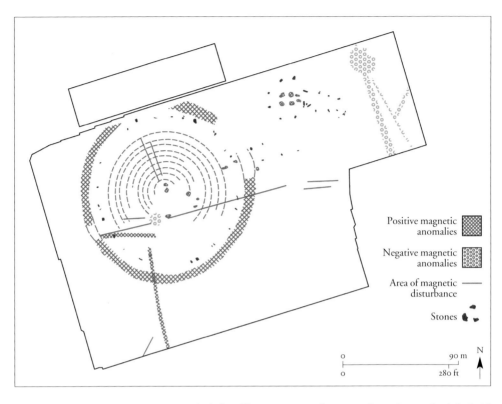

Positive magnetic
anomalies

Negative magnetic
anomalies

Area of magnetic
disturbance

Stones

0   90 m

0   280 ft

N

Plot showing the results of geomagnetic survey of Stanton Drew within the stone circle; the concentric rings of anomalies may correspond to concentric series of post-holes.

entrances slightly off-centre to northwest and southeast. Such hybrid sites have been labelled 'circle-henges', and blur the distinction drawn above between henges and stone circles. They underline the point once again that Neolithic monuments do not fall neatly into the categories that archaeologists would seek to impose on them.

One of the greatest concentrations of stone circles occurs in the southwestern peninsula of Britain, and more particularly on the uplands of Dartmoor and Bodmin Moor. There are 70 stone circles on Dartmoor and a further 16 on Bodmin Moor. Though sometimes associated with stone rows or avenues, the circles are small in scale and may be of mainly Bronze Age (2nd millennium BC) date. To their east, however, are more impressive Neolithic monuments. At Stanton Drew, close to the Bristol Channel, is a group of three stone circles in line, rather like the Thornborough henges. The largest of them, the Great Circle, measures 112 m (367 ft) across and is second only to Avebury in size. Long considered a simple (though large) ring of stones, magnetometer survey in 1997 revealed both the presence of an external ditch and no fewer than nine concentric rings of pits, ranging from 23 to 95 m (75 to 312 ft) in diameter, within the stone circle. The pits in the outer ring are estimated to be a metre in diameter and are spaced at intervals a metre apart. Some, if not all, are thought to have held timber posts. Thus Stanton Drew is a much more complex site than had been believed, and may be compared with Woodhenge (p. 117) and Mount Pleasant in Wessex, or indeed Balfarg in Scotland, where multiple timber rings stood within an enclosing circular ditch.

Timber circles leave relatively little trace, but their size and significance should not be underestimated. The depth of the post-holes at Arminghall in Norfolk suggested that they had held timber uprights 8 m (26 ft) tall. It also appears probable that in this case, the timber circle had been erected first, and only later was a henge-like bank and ditch dug around it. The aim may have been to enclose the earlier sacred structure, and restrict access to it. Once again we are struck by the process of modification to which these sites were subjected by successive generations, each modification corresponding perhaps to a shift in the meaning of the earlier monument.

The original appearance of these timber circles remains open to debate. Unlike stone circles, their uprights have long since rotted away, making it difficult to determine exactly what they looked like. Those with multiple rings of posts (such as Durrington Walls and Woodhenge) have been interpreted as roofed buildings. Such a reconstruction is unlikely for simpler structures, such as the single ring of 20 post-holes around a central multi-post feature at Sarn-y-Bryn-Caled in mid-Wales. The excavator argued that the outer ring

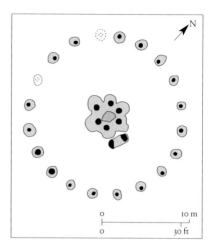

Above Post-holes mark a timber circle with central feature at Sarn-y-Bryn-Caled, mid-Wales.

Below Hypothetical reconstruction of the Sarn-y-Bryn-Caled timber circle.

may have formed a lintelled timber circle, similar to Stonehenge, but in wood. We may even envisage carved and painted posts, resembling the famous totem poles of the Northwest Coast of North America, standing at some of these sites. If they did indeed take on such an appearance, it is clear that these timber monuments would have been much more than simply timber versions of the circles built of stones.

Just 100 m (328 ft) west of the Sarn-y-Bryn-Caled timber circle was the northern terminus of a 370-m (1214-ft) long cursus; a second cursus and ring ditch lie a similar distance to the north, and there are other ring ditches in adjacent fields. The Sarn-y-Bryn-Caled circle is thus one element of a larger monument complex. This is a recurrent pattern among British Neolithic monuments. We have seen how the Thornborough site comprises three henges and two cursus monuments. At Rudston in Yorkshire, no fewer than four cursus monuments criss-cross the landscape, sometimes intersecting each other, the longest of them extending almost 4 km (2.5 miles) across undulating terrain. Still more complex is the group of monuments at Dorchester-on-Thames in southern England. The earliest monuments here were two long D-shaped enclosures, with human remains, dated 3770–3380 BC. Next (3360–3040 BC) came a 1.6-km (1-mile)

The Neolithic monument complex of Dorchester-on-Thames, Oxfordshire, with circular and rectilinear monuments side by side.

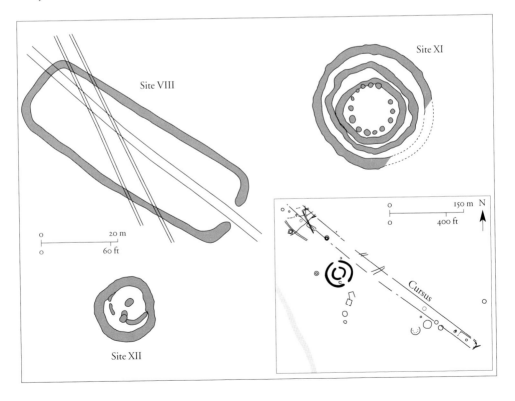

Site VIII

Site XI

Site XII

20 m
60 ft

150 m N
400 ft

Cursus

long cursus, cutting across one of the D-shaped enclosures and incorporating the other in its eastern terminal. This was followed by a series of multiple ring ditches that probably represent the remains of burial mounds, and by small ditched enclosures with external banks, a timber circle and a double-ditched henge 200 m (656 ft) in diameter. The final elements in the pattern were later ring ditches with Beaker and Early Bronze Age burials.

The clustering of monuments at certain locations indicates that these places assumed a special importance from an early stage in their development, and continued to attract new monuments over successive generations. The new monuments included both duplicates of earlier monuments (the multiple henges at Thornborough, or the cursus monuments at Rudston) and new types. Some may have been directly funerary in character (burial mounds), others intended for different kinds of ceremonies or had a different significance (henges, timber circles). Many of them were built on such a scale that they would both visibly and physically have structured the landscape. They are sufficiently numerous and closely spaced in some parts of Britain that it would have been hard to travel far without coming across a monument cluster of this kind. These were indeed monumentalized landscapes, the most famous and impressive of all being that at Avebury in southern Britain.

CHAPTER FOUR

Avebury & Stonehenge

AVEBURY AND STONEHENGE ARE PROBABLY THE MOST FAMOUS Neolithic monuments of southern Britain. Built during the 3rd millennium BC, these impressive stone circles each stand within a landscape of monuments both earlier and later in date. The sequences begin with causewayed enclosures and long mounds of the earlier Neolithic, during the middle centuries of the 4th millennium BC, and continue past the end of the Neolithic period into the Bronze Age, when clusters of round barrows were built on the surrounding ridges and uplands. The accumulation of monuments reveals the special significance that these two areas held for the communities of central southern Britain over a period of at least 2000 years.

Opposite Stonehenge: one of the sarsen trilithons at the centre of the monument.

Below Aerial view of the Avebury henge.

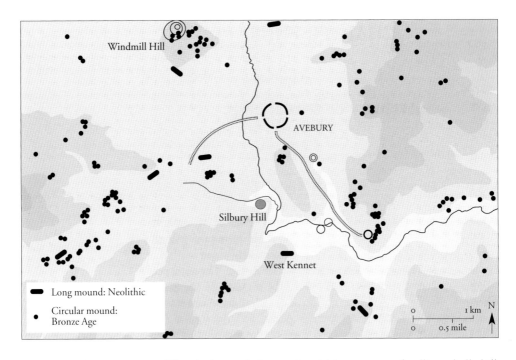

Neolithic and Bronze Age monuments in the Avebury area, including Windmill Hill, Silbury Hill and West Kennet.

The Avebury circle stands within an area of rolling chalk hills dissected by the valley of the River Kennet. Six thousand years ago, this landscape was wooded, with mature oak forests covering the chalk uplands. Farmers were just beginning to fell woodland to make clearings for their crops. By clearing the trees, they set in motion the changes which have opened up the landscape and made it what it is today. Exposed soil proved vulnerable to erosion, especially when it was ploughed and tilled, and much of it ultimately washed away into the river valley. The uplands became grassland for pasturing cattle and sheep. The first farmers, however, probably made only small clearings, which they occupied for relatively short periods. Scatters of flintwork mark the location of several Neolithic settlement sites, but no traces of buildings or houses have been discovered. There is nothing in the Avebury area to compare with the substantial timber houses of Ireland or eastern Scotland.

A 4th-millennium BC landscape

The first substantial traces of human impact on this landscape are a causewayed enclosure and a group of long mounds built during the 4th millennium BC. The long mounds include both chambered and unchambered examples, and draw attention to the fact that Avebury is in that part of Britain where traditions of megalithic and non-megalithic monuments overlap. The unchambered long mounds include those of South Street, Beckhampton Road and Horslip, excavated between 1959 and 1967. The Horslip long mound may have been built at the very beginning of the Neolithic period, in the first quarter of the 4th millennium. Beneath the South Street long mound were found criss-cross marks of ploughing by a simple ard, an early type of plough used to break up the soil for cultivation but not yet equipped with a mould board to turn the earth.

Neither the South Street long mound nor the Beckhampton Road long mound yielded any evidence of funerary activity. In neither case was there any evidence of a timber mortuary house. What the South Street mound did cover was a natural cluster of nine sarsen boulders, but whether this was some kind of shrine or sacred place remains open to debate. It raises the possibility, however, that long mounds mark locations of special importance that may not have been exclusively connected with burial.

Excavations at Beckhampton Road and South Street showed that these long mounds were no mere dumps of earth and stone, but had been constructed around a line of timber posts that ran along the long axis of the monument, with fenced bays to either side. At South Street, there were 20 pairs of bays each about 1.8 m (6 ft) wide. At Beckhampton Road, the bayed structure occupied only the eastern half of the mound, though the axial fence continued beyond this. It was also apparent that adjacent bays had in some cases received contrasting fills. This may reflect the presence of different work-groups, or an intentional desire to create contrasts within the mounds. As the excavators remarked, the yellow and brown tints of the coombe rock and brickearth would have presented a vivid contrast with the white

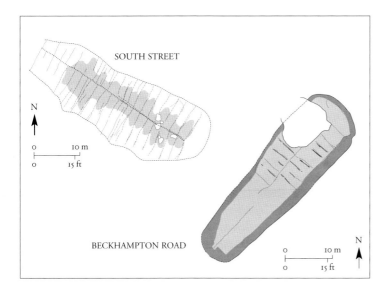

SOUTH STREET

N

0   10 m

0   15 ft

BECKHAMPTON ROAD

0   10 m

0   15 ft

N

Plans of the unchambered long mounds of Beckhampton Road and South Street, showing the systems of internal partitions.

101

marl or gravel and the dark grey turf. It is clear at all events that the builders of South Street and Beckhampton Road began by erecting a system of post-lines or fences, creating a series of separate cells, that they then filled with earth and stone to create the mound.

At about the same time that these unchambered long mounds were being built, a chambered long cairn of Cotswold-Severn type was constructed on the chalk ridge at West Kennet, overlooking Avebury from the south. This 100-m (328-ft) long mound of chalk with flanking ditches to either side is one of the best-known monuments in the Avebury area, and has already been described (p. 78). The transepted chamber contained the remains of at least 46 skeletons in varying states of disarticulation. There was also evidence that some of the bones had been removed from the chamber, perhaps for circulation among living relatives; similarly, stray long bones and skulls within the West Kennet chambers had probably been brought there from other sites. Thus the 'burial mound' of West Kennet may have been much more than a place of burial – more a locus where bodies were deposited until they had decomposed and the bones were sorted and circulated. The 'burial mounds' of South Street and Beckhampton Road, on the other hand, need not have been primarily funerary at all. It is clear, at all events, that these were not the prehistoric equivalents of modern cemeteries, intended for the definitive disposal of the dead, but were involved in more complex ritual practices.

These practices spread across the landscape to include other kinds of site, including causewayed enclosures such as Windmill Hill, northwest of Avebury. Causewayed enclosures are so called because of the interruptions, or causeways, in their ditches. The Windmill Hill causewayed enclosure consists of three circuits of ditch, one within the other, but slightly off-centre. These ditches were cut into the chalk, and the excavated material piled up to form low banks. Neither banks nor ditches, however, were continuous, and causewayed enclosures were certainly not made for defence, as was once argued. Rather, they were places for ceremonial and ritual – perhaps, among other things, for communal feasting at certain key moments in the year. Large quantities of debris and offerings were found in the ditches, left by the Neolithic communities who built and frequented this site. There were bones of several hundred animals, along with over 20,000 potsherds and approximately 100,000 pieces of worked flint. Some of this was the remains of feasting, but in the middle circuit of ditch there were skeletons of whole or partially butchered animals that must have been offerings. There were also more than 30 pieces of disarticulated human bone, almost exclusively long bones and skulls. Radiocarbon dates confirm that the activity at Windmill Hill was contemporary with that at West Kennet and at the unchambered long mounds of the area. This suggests that they should all be seen together

as interrelated parts of a single landscape of ritual practices. We cannot say for certain that the bones found at Windmill Hill came from the bodies found at West Kennet, but something like that seems very possible.

The causewayed enclosure of Windmill Hill, northwest of Avebury, with the rings of ditches interrupted by 'causeways'.

Avebury in the 3rd millennium

Similar clusters of long mounds and causewayed enclosures were to be found in several areas of southern Britain during the 4th millennium BC. Avebury was not at this stage exceptional. What followed at there during the 3rd millennium BC was, however, unique: a series of massive ritual monuments that are among the largest and most impressive of their kind.

The central focus is the Avebury henge, an enormous enclosure a little over 400 m (1312 ft) across. It is defined by a ditch, cut into the chalk to a depth of up to 10 m (33 ft) in places, with a tall bank on its outer edge. The builders had quarried an estimated 200,000 tonnes of chalk to create it. The provision of a ditch with external bank is typical of henge monuments, as we have seen, but the Avebury example is several times larger than the average British henge. It is also less regular in plan than the neatly circular henges of the type found at Thornborough, and it has four rather than two entrances. The

Some of the massive stones of the Avebury stone circle.

Avebury henge is not only one of the most massive earthworks of its type, but also encloses the largest stone circle – a ring of 98 sarsen uprights, most of them between 2 and 4 m (6.6 and 13 ft) tall. These stones were set carefully around the inner edge of the ditch. Within it again were two smaller circles, some 50 m (165 ft) across, both substantially larger in diameter than the central circle at Stonehenge. The northern inner circle is a double ring centred on an enigmatic structure known as the Cove. The three enormous sarsen blocks of the Cove are among the very largest used at Avebury. The southern circle was smaller and single, though again with a central feature – in this case a monolith known as the Obelisk. These are the principal internal features of Avebury that have been visible in recent times, but geophysical survey and aerial photographs have revealed other stone-holes, post-holes and at least one ring ditch.

The Avebury henge with its stone circles probably developed over a period

The great ditch of the Avebury henge during the excavations of the 1920s.

11 (Above) Avebury, the West Kennet avenue: the paired stones that make up this avenue leading from the Avebury henge to the Sanctuary on Overton Hill tend to alternate between wide angular shapes and taller thinner shapes, a contrast that has been likened to male and female.

12 (Below) Avebury: the Cove, a setting of two (originally three) massive blocks at the centre of the northern inner circle (visible in the background). Recent investigations have shown that the stone on the left continues at least 2 m (6.5 ft) below the surface and weighs an estimated 100 tonnes, making it by far the largest megalithic block at Avebury.

13 (Left) Part of the sarsen circle at Stonehenge, with one of the lintels still in place. Each lintel was fitted to its neighbour by a tongue-and-groove joint, and shaped to give a curved outer edge adjusted to the circumference of the circle. The careful shaping and fitting of the sarsen blocks is one of the most remarkable features of Stonehenge.

14 (Above) William Stukeley in 1723 was the first to observe that the rising sun on the midsummer solstice shone directly along the main axis into the centre of Stonehenge, but recent research suggests that the primary focus of the monument may have been in the opposite direction, towards midwinter sunset.

15 (Below) Newgrange, Ireland: the controversial reconstruction following the excavations in 1962–75 envisaged it as a cylindrical drum, with a near-vertical wall of quartz and granodiorite cobbles rising above the kerb of orthostats at the base. The cobbles may instead have been laid on the sloping surface of the cairn, or as a paved area around its foot.

16 (Opposite) The heavily decorated sillstone in front of the entrance at Newgrange is one of the most impressive examples of megalithic art, with concentric spirals interspersed with lozenges and volutes. The triple spiral motifs recurs also at the back of the chamber (see plate 19).

17 (Above) The interior of the cruciform chamber at Newgrange, looking towards the opening of the passage. At dawn on the midwinter solstice the sun's rays shine along the passage and illuminate the very rear of the chamber.

18 (Opposite below) Fourknocks, Co Meath, Ireland: the decoration on the leading edge of the capstone of the southern side cell consists of four large double lozenges with zigzags above and below.

19 (Above) Close-up of the triple spiral motif at the rear of the cruciform chamber at Newgrange.

20 Poulnabrone, western Ireland, is the most famous of the Irish portal tombs. The distinctive sloping capstone is a thin slab of local limestone. Cobbles in the foreground are the remains of the cairn which surrounded (but did not necessarily cover) the chamber.

of several centuries, though it is difficult to determine the precise chronology. The ditch and bank were created in two stages, perhaps around 3000–2900 BC. The large stone circle is somewhat later in date, and may have been added *c.* 2500 BC. The inner rings are more difficult to place in the sequence, however, and could even have preceded the digging of the main ditch. The stones themselves, some weighing over 50 tonnes, came probably from the area around Avebury, where sarsen blocks (a type of hard sandstone) lay scattered naturally across the chalk downland with clusters along valley floors. Most of these naturally occurring blocks have today been cleared for farming or used for building, but in the 3rd millennium BC the scatters of slabs and boulders would have been an impressive and mystifying sight. It is easy to see them as the direct inspiration for the circles and avenues at Avebury.

The stone-lined avenues that led from (or perhaps towards) the southern and western entrances of Avebury are one of its most remarkable features. The West Kennet avenue, marked by over 100 pairs of standing stones, still runs for 2.4 km (1.5 miles) from the southern entrance to another smaller stone ring on Overton Hill known as the Sanctuary. The Sanctuary in fact had two concentric circles of stones, the larger one 40 m (131 ft) across. Around and within the inner circle there were no fewer than six further circles

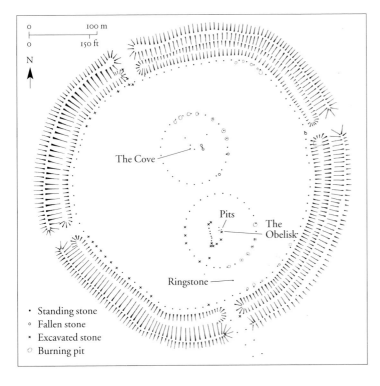

* Standing stone
○ Fallen stone
× Excavated stone
○ Burning pit

Plan of the Avebury henge, with its two internal stone circles.

113

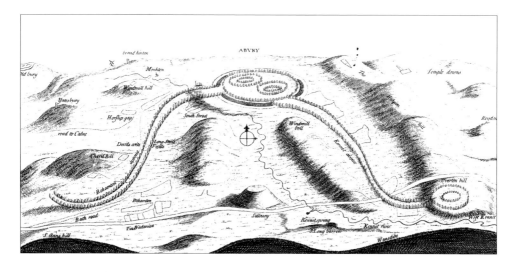

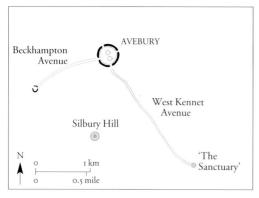

Top *Vision of the Avebury complex proposed by the antiquary William Stukeley in the early 18th century: the two avenues of standing stones are clearly shown. The Beckhampton Road avenue (left) was subsequently lost until its recent rediscovery.*

Above *The two avenues that lead from Avebury.*

of post-holes. It is unclear whether these post-holes indicate a succession of circular timber buildings on the same spot, or a single complex timber structure, but whatever the case, the stone rings probably came later. One possibility is that the timber phase of the Sanctuary was contemporary with the original henge at Avebury, around 2900 BC, and that the stone elements – the double stone ring at the Sanctuary, the outer circle at Avebury, and the West Kennet avenue that links them – represent a translation of these earth and timber concepts into stone, some three or four centuries later.

The avenue linking Avebury to the Sanctuary strongly suggests processions between the two sites. A second avenue on the western side of Avebury – the Beckhampton avenue – was recorded in the 18th century but had been lost (and its very existence doubted) until it was rediscovered in 1999. As it approached its western terminal it ran across an earlier earthwork enclosure in Longstones Field, close to the South Street long barrow, before ending at a stone setting, though one less elaborate than the stone and timber rings of the Sanctuary.

The Avebury henge and its associated avenues would be remarkable by any measure, but they are not the only 3rd-millennium monuments in the area. Indeed, in terms of work-effort the Avebury henge is dwarfed by the massive conical mound of Silbury Hill some 2 km (1.25 miles) to the south. Silbury Hill is in fact the largest humanly made prehistoric mound in Europe, 40 m (130 ft) high and 160 m (525 ft) across at its base, containing more than a third of a million cubic

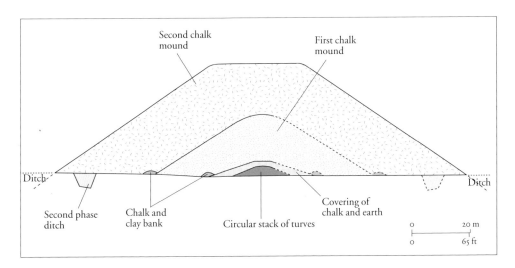

Second chalk mound

First chalk mound

Ditch

Ditch

Second phase ditch

Chalk and clay bank

Circular stack of turves

Covering of chalk and earth

0   20 m

0   65 ft

metres of chalk. At its summit is a circular level platform, 30 m (98 ft) in diameter. Excavators from the 18th century to the 1960s have searched for a burial at its centre, but failed to find any evidence of one. As a result of these explorations, however, something of the mound's internal structure is now understood. Silbury Hill is believed to have begun as a circular stack of turves, 35 m (115 ft) across and 5 m (16 ft) high. Over the top of this turf stack was raised a first chalk rubble mound, 80 m (262 ft) across and 20–25 m (66–82 ft) high. This

Above Hypothetical cross-section through Silbury Hill, based on the results of excavations by Richard Atkinson in the 1960s.

Silbury Hill today.

was followed in turn by the larger chalk rubble mound we see today, possibly originally having a stepped profile. Recent surveys have revealed a pathway spiralling up the side of the mound, though whether this is prehistoric in date remains to be established. The survey has also shown that Silbury Hill is not strictly circular in plan, but is in fact a polyhedron. An antler pick found near the summit has been dated 2490–2340 BC, suggesting that Silbury Hill may have been contemporary with the stone structures at the Avebury henge.

The purpose of Silbury Hill remains enigmatic, despite ongoing investigations. The absence of a central burial turns our attention to the summit. Was the level top the setting for observations of the night sky or simply a raised platform for special rituals? The very scale of the mound – together with the nearby henge and avenues – has fuelled speculation about Late Neolithic politics at Avebury. The size of workforce that would have been needed to raise such enormous structures has been held to argue for a hierarchy of power in this region during the 3rd millennium BC. The Avebury complex may have drawn pilgrims and adherents from across a wide area of southern Britain who perhaps assisted in the constructional projects and took part in rituals that were practised there. The absence of any richly furnished burials – or indeed of conspicuous articles of value and prestige – warns us against assuming that this was a society controlled by powerful individuals.

Avebury remained an important ritual centre after the completion of Silbury Hill and the stone circles and avenues. Around 2300 BC a series of large oval timber enclosures were built on the valley floor east of Silbury Hill. They may have been centres of ceremonial and feasting, rather like Windmill Hill a millennium and a half before, though the possibility of a defensive function cannot be ruled out. A couple of centuries later, the first of several hundred Bronze Age round barrows were raised on the chalk uplands around the Avebury enclosure. These emphasize how major Neolithic ritual centres did not simply disappear at the end of the 3rd millennium, but continued to attract new monuments in following periods. The stone settings at Avebury itself continued to be reworked; in one case (stone 41) a smaller stone was substituted for one of the original larger stones of the main circle in the early 2nd millennium BC. During the Middle Ages an attempt was made to neutralize the pagan associations of Avebury by building a church immediately outside the henge, and later by intentionally toppling and burying several of the stones. The skeleton of a 14th-century barber-surgeon was found by archaeologists accidentally crushed beneath one of the stones he had been felling. There can be no more potent testimony to the enduring power of the Avebury Neolithic complex than this attempted medieval desecration.

Stonehenge

If Avebury is the largest stone circle in Britain and Ireland, and arguably the most impressive, the most famous megalithic monument of all is without doubt Stonehenge. It shares a number of features with Avebury. It stands not in isolation, but at the heart of a complex of Neolithic monuments; it illustrates the translation of timber monuments into stone; and it remained a focus of ritual activity long after the Neolithic period had drawn formally to a close.

Stonehenge is a unique monument. Particularly distinctive are the megalithic uprights and lintels with their mortice and tenon joints, a feature borrowed from carpentry. This in itself indicates that Stonehenge marked a translation into stone of structures usually built in timber. Several neighbouring sites have concentric rings of post-holes that might have been the timber prototypes for the stone structures at Stonehenge. There were two timber circles within Durrington Walls, a henge enclosure 5 km (3 miles) east of Stonehenge that is even larger than Avebury, but without the stone circles that characterize the latter. The multiple circles of post-holes at Durrington Walls may have been roofed buildings, but they could also have been lintelled rings – like Stonehenge, but in timber. Immediately to the south of Durrington Walls, Woodhenge has a similar pattern of concentric post-rings. The Coneybury henge, 2.5 km (1.5 miles) southeast of Stonehenge, also had a timber ring within its bank and ditch. These timber circles are also generally similar in size to the central stone circle at Stonehenge.

Stonehenge.

Top *Tenons were carved at the tops of the uprights of Stonehenge to receive mortices cut in the undersides of the lintels.*

Above *Stonehenge, stone 16, showing evidence of surface treatment, perhaps in imitation of the bark of a tree.*

Another unusual feature of Stonehenge is the way that the large megalithic uprights have been shaped by a process of hammering and pounding. There are clear facets on many of the surfaces, and large numbers of hammerstones were found during excavations at Stonehenge early in the 20th century. It has been suggested that several of the stones are tooled in what might be imitation of the bark of an oak tree, while the tooling on the fallen trilithon 59 is perhaps reminiscent of beech. Thus the shaping of the stones and the finish given to their surfaces might also be making reference to the timber circles on which Stonehenge was modelled.

How are we to interpret this translation into stone of a timber circle? Stone is clearly a more durable material than wood, and structures built in stone are visibly made to last, whereas timber is a more ephemeral medium. Ethnographic analogies with the use of timber and stone in Madagascar have been evoked to suggest that the timber circles at Woodhenge and Durrington Walls may have been built for feasting and other ceremonies by the living, whereas Stonehenge was reserved for the dead.

In focusing on Stonehenge as a megalithic monument, however, there is risk of overlooking the fact that the stone elements were not present at the site in its earliest phase. The monument that we see today is indeed a culmination of multiple phases of accretion and modification extending over more than a thousand years. The first Stonehenge consisted simply of a bank with a ditch on its outer side, enclosing a circular area some 110 m (360 ft) across. This henge-type monument had a single ring of 56 substantial timber posts, marked by post-holes known as the Aubrey Holes, immediately inside the bank. There was an entrance gap to the northeast, and a further one (or more than one) to the south, but no stone elements of any kind. This phase has been dated to *c.* 2950 BC.

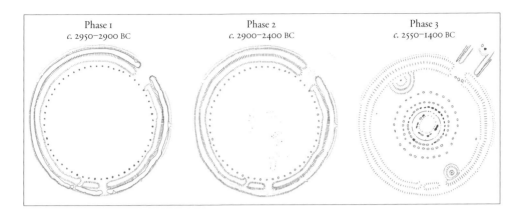

Phase 1
c. 2950–2900 BC

Phase 2
c. 2900–2400 BC

Phase 3
c. 2550–1400 BC

Nor were there any stones in the second phase at Stonehenge, when a series of timber settings were created in the interior. These might have included timber circles with lintels, rather like the later stone structures, but the interior has been too heavily disturbed to allow firm conclusions about the overall pattern. The timber posts were removed from the Aubrey Holes and cremations placed in some of them, with other cremations cut into the bank or into the filling of the ditch. Thus at this stage, in the three or four centuries following 2900 BC, Stonehenge appears to have been the locus for funerary activities, though these may have been only one part of its significance.

The three principal phases of Stonehenge. The famous stones did not arrive until the third phase.

It was during the third phase, beginning around 2550 BC, that the stones arrived at Stonehenge. They did so in two groups. First came the smaller 'bluestones', each measuring around 1.5 tonnes in weight and around 2 m (6.5 ft) tall, brought 240 km (150 miles) from the Preseli Hills in southwest Wales. They are of varied petrology (including spotted dolerite and rhyolite), but when wet they assume a distinctly bluish coloration. These blue-stones were initially set up in a double horseshoe or a double circle, forming the focus of the first megalithic Stonehenge. Subsequently, however, these bluestone settings were dismantled when the much larger sarsen blocks arrived at the site.

Transport routes by which the stones were moved to Stonehenge stones: the bluestones from southwest Wales, the sarsens from the Marlborough Downs.

The sarsen stones, weighing up to 40 tonnes, travelled a shorter distance than the bluestones, but had still to be brought approximately 30 km (18 miles) from the Marlborough Downs to the north. This in itself represents an enormous labour commitment, added to which was the effort needed to dress the stones to the required

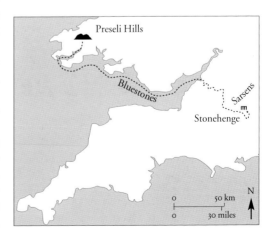

119

shape, and to raise them into position. The two principal elements of the new design were a ring of 30 uprights and 30 lintels, surrounding a central horseshoe setting of five huge trilithons. The bluestones were taken down and put to one side while the sarsen ring and the trilithon horseshoe were erected; then, when that work was complete, the bluestones were re-erected in two settings: a bluestone circle within the sarsen circle, and a bluestone oval (later modified to a horseshoe) within the trilithon horseshoe. Other sarsen monoliths were erected around the periphery of Stonehenge: two stones just outside the entrance to the northeast (including the so-called 'Heel Stone'); four others (the 'Station Stones') arranged as a rectangle within the original Stonehenge bank. At a late stage within this sequence, between 2250 and 1900 BC, the approach to Stonehenge was embellished by the provision of an avenue – not a stone-lined structure like the avenues at Avebury, but a parallel pair of banks running 2.5 km (1.5 miles) to the River Avon. It may have been a processional way, or may even have marked the route along which the bluestones had arrived at the site. The latter, given the distance they had been brought, must have held a very special significance.

The complexity of the Stonehenge sequence illustrates the recurrent process of modification and accretion to which megalithic monuments were frequently subject. Stonehenge did not reach its current form through the gradual realization of a single design over a period of several centuries. Instead, the monument appears constantly to have been rethought as successive generations added new elements or moved and removed those of their predecessors. Some of these projects were abandoned along the way: the Y and Z holes may have been dug to rearrange the bluestones in a new setting that was never completed. The key point is that monuments such as Stonehenge were not conceived as unified, finished wholes, but were always in process of becoming.

One final feature of Stonehenge illustrates this very clearly. As is well known, at dawn on the midsummer solstice the rising sun shines directly along the axis of the monument. This axis is set by the Heel Stone and its now vanished neighbour, by the midline of the avenue in its final approach to Stonehenge, and by the layout of the trilithon horseshoe at the centre of the monument. The alignment of these features is so precise that it must have been intentional. But this is a feature of the third phase of Stonehenge – the earlier phases do not appear to have followed the same axis. Thus the original northeastern entrance, defined by the break in the bank and ditch, frames a segment of the sky between 30° and 24°N, centred on 27°N. The midsummer solstice orientation of 24°N barely fits within this window, and leads us to conclude that the original Stonehenge was not aligned on the midsummer sunrise. It may have been aligned on lunar events, or it may have had no astronomical reference at all. It was only during the third phase that the northeastern entrance was widened towards the south, so that the axis of sunrise at the midsummer solstice passed through its centre. Thus solar symbolism appears only to have become important during the later modification of the monument. If we seek to determine what Stonehenge meant in the Neolithic, we are forced to conclude that there was no single fixed meaning, but rather a series of meanings changing through time.

The midsummer axis of Stonehenge was first remarked by William Stukeley in 1723, and has been much discussed ever since. It is

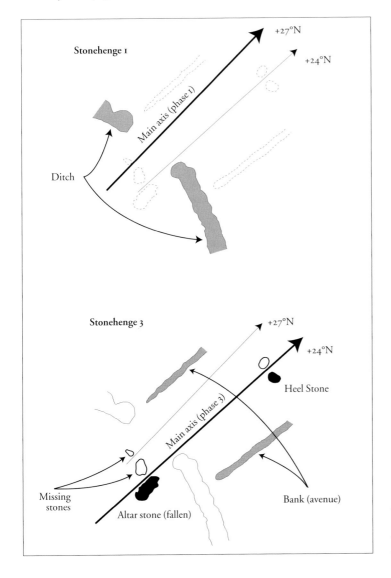

The astronomical alignment of the northeast entrance at Stonehenge in phases 1 and 3.

possible, however, that the true orientation of Stonehenge in its third phase was not towards the midsummer sunrise at all, but rather towards midwinter sunset, which occurs at precisely the opposite point of the compass. Thus the setting sun at midwinter would shine through the central trilithon of the trilithon horseshoe, full in the face of anyone who had walked into the centre of Stonehenge from the avenue and the northeast entrance. Such a focus on midwinter sunset would complement the midwinter sunrise alignment observed at passage graves such as Maes Howe and Newgrange.

Stonehenge, like Avebury, was not an isolated monument, but stands within a landscape of prehistoric monuments of varying kinds. Around the middle of the 4th millennium BC, before Stonehenge was begun, there was a cluster of six long barrows to the southwest and a causewayed enclosure known today as Robin Hood's Ball some 4 km (2.5 miles) to the north. By the end of the 4th millennium two cursus monuments (the Stonehenge Cursus and the Lesser Cursus) had been constructed on the low ground north of the small ridge where the first Stonehenge was soon to be built. During the following centuries, perhaps contemporary with the second phase Stonehenge (with internal timber structures), the large henge at Durrington Walls and the smaller timber circles at Coneybury and Woodhenge were built. At this stage, Stonehenge was just one of several earth and timber circles in the region, and the enclosed area was much smaller than that of Durrington Walls. It was only in the third stage, with the arrival of the

Reconstruction of Woodhenge proposed by Stuart Piggott.

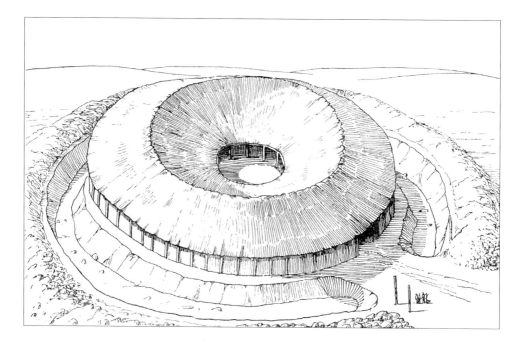

bluestones and sarsens, that Stonehenge became the most elaborate monument of the entire area. As such, like Avebury, it attracted numerous Bronze Age burial mounds in the centuries that followed, arranged in rows along the ridges overlooking it.

One spectacular recent discovery is the grave of the 'Amesbury Archer' at Boscombe Down, 3 km (2 miles) from Stonehenge. This grave pit (which may have been timber-lined, and covered by a small turf mound) contained the skeleton of a 35–45 year-old man. Oxygen isotope analysis of his teeth indicated that as a child he had lived in mainland Europe. The grave also held archer's equipment (15 finely flaked flint barbed-and-

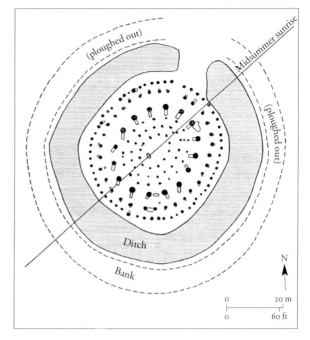

tanged arrowheads and two polished stone wristguards), three decorated Beaker vessels, three copper knives, a pair of gold hair ornaments, a shale belt ring and a black 'cushion stone' for metalworking. This is the 'richest' Beaker grave so far found in Britain.

A second grave, discovered nearby, contained the crouched skeleton of a younger male, accompanied by gold hair ornaments of the very same style. An inherited abnormality of the foot bones suggests that these two individuals were closely related, perhaps even father and son. The particular significance of these burials is indicated by the radiocarbon dates of 2400–2200 BC, which suggest that these men may have been alive at the time that the megalithic structures of Stonehenge were being built. In this later part of the Stonehenge sequence, therefore, we may at last have evidence for societies in which the status and prestige of leading individuals were being directly displayed.

Another grave of the same period has been found nearby, once again in the area to the east of Stonehenge. It contained the remains of three adult men, three children and one young adult, accompanied by 7 or 8 Beaker vessels. Together they have been called the 'Boscombe Bowmen' from the five barbed-and-tanged flint arrowheads that were found in the grave. The adults and the young adult share specific features of skull morphology, suggesting that they were a family group. The most remarkable finding, however, comes from strontium isotope analysis of the teeth, which this time shows that the three

Plan of Woodhenge showing the concentric rings of post-holes enclosed within a circular ditch and bank.

123

Below *Gold hair ornaments of the 'Amesbury Archer'.*

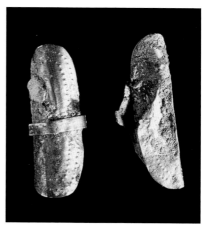

The 'Amesbury Archer', a single inhumation accompanied by flint arrowheads, archer's wristguards, copper knives, gold ornaments and Beaker vessels.

adults had been born either in the Lake District or Wales, and had migrated to Wessex when they were between 3 and 13 years old.

Were these men connected with the transport of the bluestones to Stonehenge from the Preseli Hills? This intriguing scenario reminds us once again how the significance of major centres such as Stonehenge and Avebury may have resonated over wide areas of southern Britain, far beyond their immediate environs, attracting people from distant lands.

CHAPTER FIVE

Ireland

IRELAND HAS A RANGE OF NEOLITHIC MONUMENTS THAT OVERLAP TO some degree with those of Britain, but have their own regional identities. The Irish Neolithic as a whole must not be considered simply an extension of that of Britain, still less of the 'classic' region of southern England. Ireland, along with Scotland, Wales and northern England, had its own specific patterns of settlement and cultural practice during the Neolithic. The chambered tombs of Ireland, for example, are somewhat different from those of Britain, both in their morphology and their landscape placement, and in the practices that were associated with them. The most famous Irish monuments are the megalithic tombs, stone circles and alignments, of which there are several hundred, but to these must be added a number of earthwork monuments and a growing list of Neolithic palisade enclosures, especially in the north and east. These monuments must be understood against a background of varying terrain, from coastal cliffs and denuded limestone uplands in the west to the low-lying lakes and bogs of the centre and the rolling clay-capped hills of the east.

Houses and fields

One important difference between Ireland and southern Britain is the relative abundance in Ireland of Neolithic houses. In southern Britain, the rarity of house remains has been used to argue for a model of a mobile Neolithic, in direct continuity with the preceding Mesolithic, in which livestock husbandry played a more significant role than cereal cultivation. The basis for this model even for southern Britain may be open to question, but in Ireland the settlement evidence suggests a very different picture. Two varieties of house structure have been discovered: rectangular houses, dated to the Irish Early Neolithic (4000–3600 BC); and less substantial circular houses, which became the dominant type during the Middle and Late Neolithic. Some 40 rectangular houses are now known from Ireland, most of them with bedding trenches for walls of plank-built

Opposite *Ballyglass, Co. Mayo: a court cairn with two megalithic chambers both opening on to a central space (court) accessed by an entrance on the northeast side of the oval cairn. The northern end of the cairn covers the remains of a rectangular Neolithic house, represented by post-holes and bedding trenches for the walls.*

construction. These were large buildings, varying from 6 to almost 14 m (20– 46 ft) in length and up to 8 m (26 ft) in width. At some sites, several such houses are clustered together, and certain of them, such as Ballyharry 1, show evidence of rebuilding, which indicates that they were occupied for a long enough period to require repair. A number of them are directly associated with megalithic monuments. At Ballyglass in northwest Ireland, a large rectangular house was demolished to make way for the construction of a megalithic tomb of 'court cairn' type; while at Knowth, remains of four rectangular houses were found, one of them directly beneath the passage of the western passage grave in the main mound. Were these houses 'special' buildings that were demolished to make way for the tombs, or were they 'ordinary' domestic dwellings? It is hard to be sure.

The later, smaller circular houses are perhaps more readily interpreted as 'normal' domestic dwellings, though these too are sometimes associated with megalithic structures. Traces of nine circu-

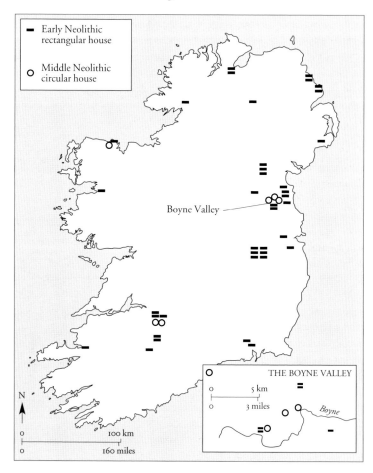

Map showing the distribution of Neolithic houses (circular and rectangular) in Ireland.

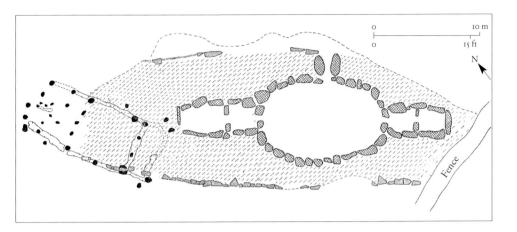

lar buildings at Knowth had the same type of pottery – Carrowkeel ware – as the passage tombs, although the passage tombs were built over the house sites. At nearby Townleyhall, stake-built circular houses preceded the construction of a passage grave. The continuing currency of this house type is shown at Newgrange, where a cluster of small circular houses was built around the southwestern edge of the mound at the very end of the Neolithic, around 2200 BC, associated with Beaker pottery.

For the landscapes of daily life we can turn to locations in the west of Ireland where Neolithic field systems have been exposed. The most famous of these is Céide fields in County Mayo. Here a system of dry-stone walls extending 5 km (3 miles) along the coast and covering 1000 ha (2470 acres) has been discovered beneath the blanket bog (p. 11). In the western part of the area, the dry-stone walls define a series of narrow linear strips running towards the cliffs, with transverse walls subdividing them into smaller units. Plough marks were found in one location and pollen evidence suggests that the fields were used for cereal cultivation. Also associated with the fields were a number of megalithic tombs, probably built by the same people as those who laid out and worked the fields. A similar field system with associated court cairns has been found at Rathlackan to the east, and megalithic tombs are located within a less orderly system of dry-stone walls at Roughaun Hill in County Clare, some 150 km (90 miles) to the south.

Below *Neolithic field system and chambered tombs on Roughan Hill, Co. Clare.*

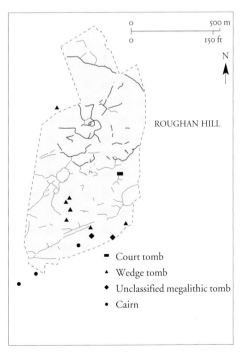

ROUGHAN HILL

- ■ Court tomb
- ▲ Wedge tomb
- ◆ Unclassified megalithic tomb
- • Cairn

This integration of megalithic tombs within a system of Neolithic houses and field walls is unique in western Europe, and for the moment is limited to these coastal areas of western Ireland. It shows that the tombs were connected to stable settlement systems based on mixed arable cultivation and livestock husbandry. Were other regions of Ireland and Britain once the same, with houses and fields present from the very start of the Neolithic? Might it be just that the evidence is better preserved in western Ireland? Or was the character of Neolithic settlement completely different in other parts of Ireland or indeed in most of Britain? The current consensus favours the latter conclusion: that we should not be thinking in terms of a single, uniform Neolithic, established throughout Britain and Ireland, but of many regional variants. There is no reason to believe that Neolithic life in western Ireland was lived in the same way as it was in Wessex or on Orkney. This implies that Neolithic monuments may have operated in very different ways in different regions. That indeed is exactly what the diversity in both the kinds of monuments and the evidence for their use would lead us to conclude.

Classifying the tombs

Irish megalithic tombs have traditionally been divided into four principal categories: passage tombs; court cairns; portal tombs; and wedge tombs. To these may be added the less ambitious but still monumental Linkardstown cists, and the less formal 'boulder burials'. While the different tomb types can often be easily distinguished, the chronological evidence indicates that passage tombs, court cairns and portal tombs were largely contemporary with each other; only wedge tombs form a separate, somewhat later category (and 'boulder burials' appear to be later still). Furthermore, though some types are more common in certain regions and are absent from others, they overlap geographically. Passage tombs, for example, are mainly concentrated in the northern half of Ireland, but are also found more rarely in the south and even the southwest. Similar mortuary practices are also spread across the different tomb types, with cremation playing a significant role at passage tombs and at certain court cairns.

A good place to start is once again in western Ireland, at the megalithic cemetery of Carrowmore. Here a cluster of some 60 tombs is arranged in an oval ring measuring 1 km (0.6 mile) across from north to south. Each tomb consists of a small boulder-built megalithic chamber within a boulder circle. They do not have passages and may not have had covering mounds, and in both respects stand out as somewhat atypical within the corpus of Irish megalithic tombs as a whole. The exception is Carrowmore tomb 51, which is located at the centre of the space defined by the oval. This too is

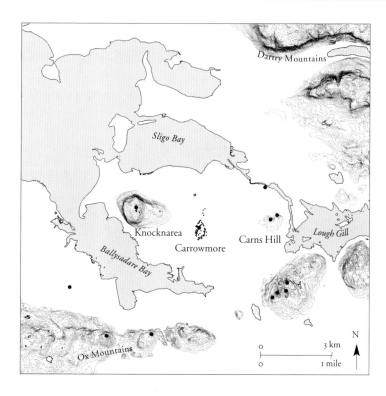

Neolithic chambered tombs around Carrowmore, Co. Sligo: the Carrowmore cemetery lies within a plain surrounded by the Ox Mountains, Carns Hill and Knocknarea, on which were built a series of passage graves (indicated by black dots); the monuments of Carrowmore itself are arranged in a ring around a larger monument covered by a cairn (monument 51).

Tomb no. 7 at Carrowmore: a chamber built of large blocks surrounded by a boulder circle.

*Passage tombs beneath
circular cairns in the
Carrowkeel cemetery,
Co. Sligo.*

surrounded by a boulder circle, but it is distinguished from the other Carrowmore tombs both by the presence of a covering cairn and by the form and construction of the chamber: a rectangular megalithic structure covered by a massive limestone slab. Tomb 51 is also the only one at Carrowmore to contain inhumations (rather than cremations) and the only one to have megalithic art (a row of circles on the leading edge of the capstone). Radiocarbon dates show that tomb 51 was probably the last of the Carrowmore tombs to be built, around 3500 BC. Thus this slab-built megalithic chamber with covering cairn comes late in the sequence.

How much earlier the other Carrowmore tombs may be has been the subject of some debate. Radiocarbon dates obtained in the 1970s suggested that they were among the earliest megalithic tombs in western Europe. It was argued that they might even have been built by local hunter-gatherer groups before they began to adopt agriculture: that they were in fact Mesolithic megaliths. The chronological evidence has, however, been reassessed, and it is now generally accepted that the Carrowmore tombs belong to the Irish Early Neolithic (*c.* 4000–3600 BC). They may date to the very beginning of that period, but no earlier. Thus in Ireland, as in Britain, the construction of the earliest monuments appears to follow closely after the transition from Mesolithic to Neolithic.

The cemetery-like clustering of tombs at Carrowmore is a recurrent feature of the Irish Neolithic. The three major passage tomb cemeteries are those of Carrowkeel (not far from Carrowmore), Loughcrew (in central Ireland) and Brú na Bóinne (the Bend of the Boyne, in eastern Ireland, north of Dublin). Carrowkeel consists of an impressive set of cairns positioned on a series of prominent ridges and spurs. Loughcrew, in somewhat gentler terrain, has passage tombs arranged in three interlinked clusters on adjacent hilltops, overlooking a cursus monument and standing stones on the lower ground to its north. The Brú na Bóinne cemetery likewise exploits hilltops and ridges to give the greatest possible prominence to its monumental passage tombs (see below).

Court cairns

Prominence was apparently a less important consideration in the location of other Irish Neolithic tombs. Portal tombs and court cairns tend to be placed not on hilltops, but on the middle or lower slopes.

Court cairns are a distinctive Irish tomb type in which an open space or courtyard is framed within the projecting arms of an elongated dry-stone cairn. The court tomb is essentially a development of the horned cairn, where the chamber opens from the middle of a concave façade. It is, however, the more elaborated examples which give their name to the specifically Irish type. One of the best preserved court cairns is at Creevykeel in western Ireland. Here the outer envelope takes the form of a trapezoidal dry-stone cairn some 70 m (230ft) long. A narrow entrance passage in the middle of the broader eastern end leads into an oval courtyard faced with low orthostats. Immediately ahead, a row of slightly larger orthostats (the largest 1.8 m/6 ft tall) frame the entrance to the burial chamber, which consists of an elongated space divided by a portal half way along its length. The entrance is covered by a megalithic lintel, though towards the back of the chamber there was evidence of corbelling and the chamber itself may originally have been covered by a corbelled vault. There is no formal passage leading into the chamber – this is not a passage tomb –

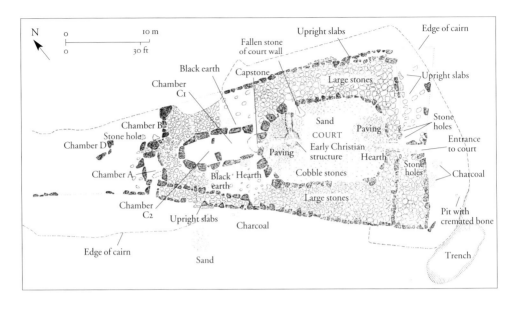

N

0   10 m

0   30 ft

Fallen stone of court wall

Upright slabs

Edge of cairn

Black earth

Capstone

Large stones

Upright slabs

Chamber C1

Sand

Paving

Stone holes

Chamber B

COURT

Entrance to court

Stone hole

Chamber D

Early Christian structure

Paving

Hearth

Chamber A

Black earth

Hearth

Cobble stones

Stone holes

Charcoal

Chamber C2

Upright slabs

Large stones

Pit with cremated bone

Charcoal

Edge of cairn

Sand

Trench

The court cairn of Creevykeel, Co. Sligo.

although the entrance is narrower than the chamber beyond. In the tail of the cairn, behind the main chamber, are traces of three (perhaps originally four) supplementary chambers, small polygonal structures with short passages, opening symmetrically from each long side.

The most distinctive feature of Creevykeel is the central court, an open space measuring 17 m (56 ft) long by 10 m (33 ft) wide, and originally paved. Horned cairns are found in other parts of Britain, but only in Ireland do the horns develop to the extent that they completely enclose the forecourt. The effect would have been to shield and conceal from the outside world any rituals that were being carried out there – to create a hidden and isolated arena. At Creevykeel remains of four cremated individuals were found in the chamber, and at another court cairn, Ballymarlagh in Antrim, traces of the funeral pyre were found within the court itself. So the court may have been the place where the dead were transformed from corpses to ashes and burned bones, which were then placed in the chamber.

Court tombs are restricted to the northern half of Ireland. Their origins may lie in still earlier timber monuments. The simple elongated chambers with internal partition resemble the mortuary houses found beneath British long mounds. A mortuary house of this kind was found at Dooey's Cairn at Ballymacaldrack, northeast Ireland. The Dooey's Cairn mortuary house was deliberately burned and was incorporated subsequently within a dry-stone cairn with megalithic façade and chamber. Court cairns also share features with the Clyde cairns of southwest Scotland. Thus although court cairns are unique to Ireland, some of their elements have parallels in other regions: the internal court developing from horned kinds of the type found also in Scotland; the elongated chamber related perhaps to timber mortuary houses. Nowhere else, however, do we find internal courts in which in all likelihood the mortuary rituals were performed.

Interpretation by Gabriel Cooney of the sequence of construction and successive modifications at Dooey's Cairn, Co. Antrim: a timber mortuary house is later monumentalized by the construction of a cairn, which is in turn transformed into a court cairn; the court was eventually infilled by a deposit of dry stone.

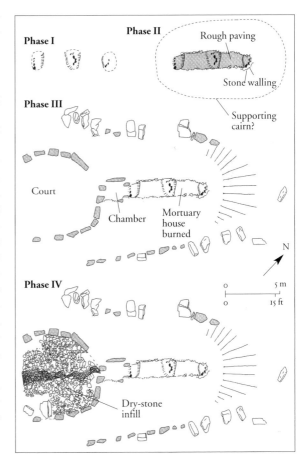

Phase I

Phase II

Rough paving

Stone walling

Phase III

Supporting cairn?

Court

Chamber

Mortuary house burned

N

Phase IV

0   5 m
0   15 ft

Dry-stone infill

Portal tombs

The denuded upland plateau of the Burren lies 160 km (100 miles) south of Creevykeel. Here are found some of the most spectacular examples of another Irish tomb type, the portal tomb. The Burren is an area of exposed limestone pavement, and the portal tombs were built by levering up the thin limestone slabs of the eroded bedrock and setting them on end among the natural parallel fissures. Other slabs were then extracted and placed as capstones on the uprights. Portal tombs have a distinctive profile, with parallel sides increasing in height towards the entrance, the shape emphasized by the conspicuous oversailing capstone. The massive portal stones support one end of the capstone, with a sill stone between them at ground level across the entrance. In longer examples there may be two capstones and seven or eight orthostats, but in all cases the capstones slope downwards towards the back of the tomb. There is no passage, and, as with the similar tombs of southwestern Britain, the presence of a covering mound or cairn has sometimes been disputed: the striking appearance of the sloping capstones, it has been argued, was surely not made to be hidden. In many cases, however, there are traces of a long cairn in which the chamber must have stood, though it is possible that the cairn was a kind of platform and did not entirely cover the chamber.

Portal tombs are found in two distinct areas of Ireland: in mid-Ulster in the north, and in an east–west band across the centre of the country from Dublin to Sligo, ending at the Burren. The most famous of the portal tombs on the Burren is at Poulnabrone, where the thin limestone capstone rests on a pair of portal slabs 1.8 m (6 ft) tall with a lower second and third pair of orthostats behind, sloping sharply down towards the rear. Around it are the remains of an oval cairn some 9 m (30 ft) across. Within the chamber was a large quantity of disarticulated human remains from at least 16 adults and 6 children. Radiocarbon dates on these remains gave a wide range of dates, from the early part of the 4th millennium BC (4050–3700 BC) to around 3200 BC. It is possible that the human remains at Poulnabrone were deposited over a period of several centuries. If the earliest of the dates fix the construction of the tomb, then Poulnabrone must have been built in the early 4th millennium BC. The relatively simple character of the chamber – an elongated rectangular box – recalls the chambers of court cairns, and suggests that portal and court tombs each developed from the same point of departure. In the case of court cairns, it was the cairn that became more elaborate; in the case of portal tombs, the chamber.

Passage tombs

The third major type of chambered tomb in 4th millennium Ireland was the passage tomb. Passage tombs are found mainly in the north, where they are often placed in prominent hill top locations. The most famous of the passage tombs are those in the band of cemeteries across the centre of the country from Brú na Bóinne (the Boyne valley) in the east to Carrowkeel in the west. The simple polygonal chambers of the Carrowmore cemetery may be ancestral to early Irish passage tomb forms, and there is certainly good evidence to suggest that the earliest Irish passage tombs were small. The large and impressive examples of Dowth, Knowth and Newgrange are the outcome of several hundred years of Irish passage tomb development.

At the same time, passage tombs in Ireland, as elsewhere, are part of a more widespread Atlantic phenomenon; the Irish examples did not develop in isolation. This much is suggested by parallels between the megalithic art of the Boyne valley tombs and megalithic art in Britain and Brittany, though the Boyne valley art is probably several centuries later in date. The Boyne valley tombs also demonstrate how in Ireland as in Britain, Neolithic monuments of different types occur in close proximity, creating what are essentially monumentalized ritual landscapes.

Neolithic monuments of Brú na Bóinne, Boyne valley, Co. Meath.

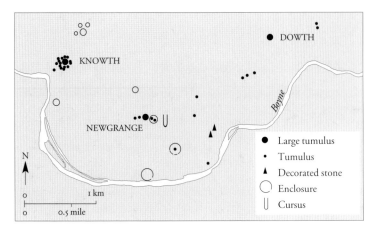

The Boyne valley complex

Along with Avebury and Orkney, Brú na Bóinne forms one the key monument complexes of Neolithic Britain and Ireland. The River Boyne rises in the hill country west of Dublin and flows 110 km (68 miles) northwards and then eastwards before debouching into the Irish Sea. Some 20 km (12 miles) before reaching its destination, the river's easterly course is blocked by a low ridge which forces it to flow southwards in a broad curve, so creating the Bend of the Boyne or 'Brú na Bóinne'. It is on this ridge towards the end of the 4th millennium BC that three large and impressive passage tomb mounds were constructed: Dowth, Knowth and Newgrange.

Travelling upstream from the east, the first monument to be encountered is Dowth, a flattened grassy hummock some 85 m (278 ft) in diameter. This is the least well known of the three main passage grave mounds, but it resembles Knowth and Newgrange in the presence of an encircling kerb, internal chambers and megalithic art. Only around half of the kerbstones at Dowth are visible, comprising 66 stones of which 15 are decorated with pecked and engraved motifs. The two passage tombs in this mound, which have further decorated stones, are unlike the passage tombs at Knowth and Newgrange in that they intrude only a limited way into the western flank of the mound. The northern chamber has a cruciform plan (with a curious southern annex) and stone basins similar to those found at Knowth

One of the two chambers of Dowth, one of the large passage tombs in the Brú na Bóinne cemetery.

and Newgrange. The southern chamber is unusual in being circular in plan but it shares with Newgrange the feature that the sun's rays shine directly into the chamber at dawn on the winter solstice.

Newgrange: the controversial reconstruction of the main façade.

Continuing upstream around the Bend of the Boyne, the gleaming white façade of Newgrange comes next into view. Following excavations between 1962 and 1975, the mound of Newgrange has been reconstructed as a flattened cylinder 85 m (278 ft) across and over 13 m (43 ft) high. An entrance in the southeastern side gives access to a long megalithic passage leading to a spectacular corbel-vaulted chamber some 6 m (20 ft) high. The impact is enhanced by the relative lowness of the passage, which at its outer end is only 1.5 m (5 ft) high. The chamber itself is of cruciform plan, with large stone basins in each of its three arms (in fact, two of them in the eastern recess). Newgrange is one of the megalithic tombs for which we possess an early written description. It was visited in 1699 by Welsh antiquary Edward Lhwyd not long after its discovery. The advantages of possessing such an early account must be weighed against the disadvantages of the subsequent damage which 300 years of visitors have exacted. The excavations of the 1960s and 1970s nonetheless succeeded in recovering the remains of several cremated individuals within the chamber, plus two scattered inhumations. It is possible that the two rites were practised concurrently; though it is more likely that the inhumations were added at a later date.

Aside from its impressive corbelled vault it is the number of decorated stones at Newgrange that have excited particular interest. The kerb around the base of the mound is composed of 97 slabs, mostly of greywacke from deposits a few kilometres to the north. Of the 97 kerbstones, 31 bear pecked and engraved designs, with lozenges, chevrons, zigzags, circles and spirals the commonest motifs. Where the marks are especially deep or broad, they have often been smoothed with a pebble. The most elaborate of all the designs are those executed in raised relief, where the background has been pecked away to leave the motif standing out. This is the technique used on the massive entrance stone (K1), and on the elaborately decorated stone (K52) at the diametrically opposite point on the back of the mound. These were evidently positions of special significance in the kerb. Most of the kerbstones, by contrast, have relatively simple designs – a few roughly pecked spirals, a couple of meandering or zigzag lines. Further decorated stones form parts of the passage and chamber, and some of these had clearly been carved before their installation as they have designs on their edges or their hidden rear faces. It is possible, indeed, that they were taken from an earlier megalithic tomb on this spot.

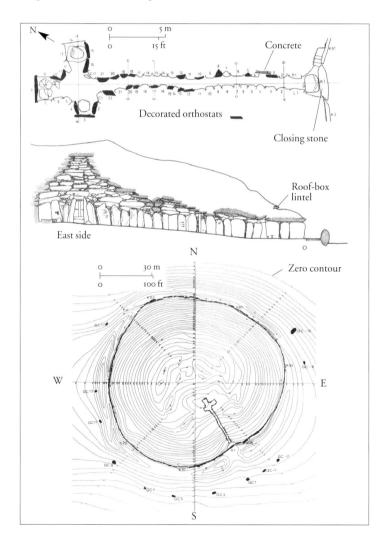

Newgrange: the cruciform passage tomb within its circular cairn.

The megalithic art of Newgrange has long been admired, but it was a discovery in the 1960s that added a new dimension to our understanding of the site. It had been known since the 1840s that above and behind the entrance to the passage there was a decorated lintel. In 1963 this was revealed to be the top of a narrow slot that allowed light to shine directly into the tomb along the passage. The angle of this slot – the so-called 'roof-box' – had been carefully engineered so that at midwinter solstice the rays of the rising sun shone directly along the passage to illuminate the back of the cruciform chamber (see p. 20). Given that the floor of the chamber is some 2 m (6.6 ft) above the ground level outside the passage entrance, and that the roof-box itself is 2 m (6.6 ft) in length, it was a remarkable achievement on the part of the Neolithic builders to have designed and built the structure to such a high degree of accuracy. The symbolism of midwinter solstice must have been powerfully significant. Perhaps this particular sunrise, on the darkest day of the year, was associated with ideas of rebirth or resurrection as the sun's rays illuminated the innermost part of the tomb.

The reconstructed Newgrange façade – a near-vertical wall of white with black inclusions – draws on evidence from the excavations. A layer of white quartz blocks and dark grey granite boulders extended outwards for a distance of 6–7 m (20–23 ft) from the kerb,

A circle of standing stones was built around Newgrange at the end of the Neolithic.

The large decorated slab before the entrance to the tomb of Newgrange.

but this layer was only present along the southeastern side of the mound, in front of the entrance. The excavator believed that the blocks were the collapsed remains of a tall façade that had stood either side of the tomb entrance. It is more likely, however, that the quartz and granite had simply been spread on the ground to form a stone pavement in front of the tomb. Recent geological studies have identi-fied the source of the materials involved: the quartz came from the Wicklow Mountains, 40 km (25 miles) to the south; the granite from Dundalk Bay, 35 km (21 miles) to the north (p. 15). Both these materials were present in such large quantities that an enormous effort of transport must have been required to collect them and bring them to Newgrange. Nor must we overlook the labour of transporting the substantial kerbstones. Though they may only have travelled 5 km (3 miles) or so, none of them weighs less than a tonne. The building of tombs such as this would have been beyond the capacity of single small communities, yet there is no clear evidence of powerful individuals or centralized authority at this period. How, then, did the passage tomb cemeteries come to be built? Were they sacred places, drawing people together from across wide areas of 4th millennium Ireland?

Proceeding further round the Bend of the Boyne, the third major tomb in this complex is Knowth, a massive circular mound closely hedged round by a cluster of smaller passage tombs. Of similar dimen-sions to Dowth and Newgrange, the main mound at Knowth is in some senses more spectacular than either. In the first place, it contains not one but two large passage tombs, arranged back to back; and sec-ondly, these two passage tombs, together

Corbelled vault of the eastern passage tomb at Knowth.

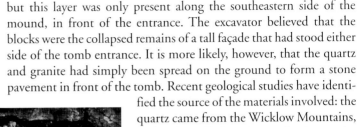

Left *Knowth: stone basin in the northern arm of the eastern passage tomb; note the decoration of megalithic art on the internal surface of the basin.*

with the kerb that encircles the mound, incorporate more than 300 decorated stones. Knowth has the greatest concentration of megalithic art in western Europe. The western passage tomb is of 'undifferentiated' type – the passage simply ends in a wider and taller terminal that forms the chamber. The eastern passage tomb is of cruciform type, with corbel-vaulted roof and stone basins in the terminal cell and the southern side-cell. The dead had been mainly cremated, as at Newgrange, though the remains were much better preserved and the numbers recorded were accordingly much greater. The larger eastern passage tomb had evidence of around 100 individuals. Along with these human remains were found a small number of remarkable prestige objects, including a finely carved ceremonial macehead and a decorated bone or antler pin that may have come from Iberia. These show that important centres such as this may have stood as nodes within a web of interregional connections.

Around the main mound at Knowth are no fewer than 17 satellite mounds, most with passage tombs of undifferentiated or cruciform plan. Like the main

Above Knowth, Brú na Bóinne: the northwestern sector of the central mound during excavations. Several of the kerbstones are decorated with megalithic art.

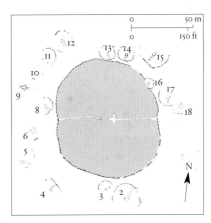

Above Knowth: plan of the central cairn (site 1) encircled by satellite passage tombs.

Satellite cairns at Knowth.

mound, they contained remains of cremated individuals, along with occasional grave offerings. The passages of the satellite tombs for the most part faced towards the main mound, though some (such as site 13) were so close against its kerb that access would have been difficult. This suggests that the satellite tombs preceded the construction of the main mound, at least in its final form. Site 16, indeed, was subsequently incorporated into the main mound, and the kerb of the latter is flattened to avoid site 13, so we can be sure that these two satellite mounds were already in existence when the main mound was built. Only two of the satellite tombs (sites 17 and 18) appear to post-date the main mound, and it is possible that all the others precede it. This would have meant that at an early stage in the development of Knowth, there would have been a ring of satellite tombs with their passages facing inwards towards the empty space where the main mound was subsequently to be built. What stood in this empty space? Study of the engraved orthostats from the western passage tomb at Knowth has indicated that they were placed upside down, and hence must have been re-used from an earlier structure. It is possible that they came from an early decorated passage tomb that was later demolished to make way for the present main mound of Knowth. Something similar may have happened at Newgrange.

The satellite tombs are not the earliest traces of Neolithic activity at Knowth. As we saw earlier (p. 126), two rectangular houses had been built here at the very beginning of the Neolithic, followed a little later by a sub-rectangular structure and by ten or so circular houses. All of these precede the first of the passage tombs. Nor were the passage tombs the end of the sequence at Knowth: a timber circle was built to the east of the main mound during the Late Neolithic. Thus the main tomb at Knowth is merely the largest element in a cluster of activity that includes lesser monuments (the satellite passage tombs) and extends in time from the beginning to the end of the Neolithic.

The same is true of Dowth and Newgrange. At Newgrange, the main mound stands at the centre of a low ridge with two smaller passage tombs (sites K and L) to the west, and one or possibly two more (sites Z and Z1) to the east. The latter were built on ground that had been stripped for turf to build the main mound, and they must hence post-date its construction. A further passage tomb (site A) lay downslope, between Newgrange and the river. Site A was later encircled by an earthen ring, and a second such ring was built on the river bank to the west. A still larger earthen ring was built to the east of Dowth, while a fourth, together with a clay-lined ritual pond, exists at Monknewtown, 2 km (1.25 miles) to the north. Upslope, cutting across the eastern end of the Newgrange ridge, is a cursus, with parallel banks 100 m (328 ft) long ending at a U-shaped terminal overlooking the river. Later still, towards the end of the Neolithic

period, a circle of timber posts was built to the south of the main mound at Newgrange, encircling passage tomb Z. Within the post-ring were concentric rings of pits filled with the debris of feasting. It is clear from all this that Newgrange remained a focus of ceremonial and symbolic importance long after the tomb itself had ceased to be used for burials. Later still, the main mound was enclosed within a circle of standing stones, and a cluster of small circular houses (with Beaker-type pottery) was built up against its kerb.

Thus the Neolithic monument complex at the Bend of the Boyne consists not just of the three main mounds, but also of up to 40 passage tombs plus a series of embanked earthwork enclosures, a cursus, several post-rings and a stone circle. The passage tombs belong to the later 4th millennium BC (radiocarbon dates from Knowth and Newgrange suggest between 3200 and 2900 BC), but were preceded by Early Neolithic settlement activity reaching back to 4000 BC, and they were followed by ritual activity extending down to the end of the 3rd millennium BC. This long sequence indicates the continuing importance of this specific location throughout the Neolithic period. It also illustrates its changing scale and character, from domestic, to

Excavation in progress at Knowth. Some of the 17 satellite passage tombs are visible as mounds; others have been excavated down to their foundations.

funerary, to feasting and ceremonial. Like Stonehenge, such places did not have a fixed, immutable significance, but shifted their meaning as successive generations interpreted and reinterpreted the monuments of their forebears.

Linkardstown cists, wedge tombs and boulder burials

The Boyne valley tombs are the largest and most impressive Neolithic monuments in Ireland. At the other end of the scale, and only slightly earlier in date, are the modest megalithic structures known as Linkardstown cists.

In contrast to passage tombs, portal tombs and court cairns, Linkardstown cists are restricted to an area of southern Ireland from Limerick in the west to Wicklow in the east. They are simple in structure and lack an entrance passage, consisting essentially of a slab-built chamber of polygonal or rectangular plan under a circular or oval mound. The Ashleypark burial had a trapezoidal chamber containing the remains of three disarticulated individuals, which was concealed within a clay mound that was in turn surrounded by a pair of concentric ditches with external banks. One of the individuals was an adult male; the others were children of 4–5 years and 1 year old respectively. Some Linkardstown cists contain only a single individual, not always disarticulated. The fact that these are usually adult males may indicate that they were the burial places for high-ranking individuals. Hence the Linkardstown cists are fundamentally different in character from the collective burials of court, portal or passage tombs. The closed chambers of Linkardstown cists would have limited repeated access, and there was an emphasis on individual rather than multiple interments. Chronologically, however, they lie within the later 4th millennium BC and are thus contemporary with court cairns, portal tombs and passage tombs. Radiocarbon dating indeed suggests they had a fairly short currency between *c.* 3550 and 3350 BC.

The Linkardstown cists add to the diversity of tomb types that were being built in Ireland during the later 4th millennium BC. By the middle of the 3rd millennium, however, most of these were no longer being constructed or used. But Irish tomb-building did not end with the Boyne valley passage tombs of the late 4th millennium BC. Towards the close of the Neolithic and into the Early Bronze Age, a new type of chamber tomb made its appearance: the wedge tomb.

The wedge tombs of western Ireland are the most numerous of all Irish megalithic tomb types, and among the latest in date. The southwestern counties of Cork and Kerry have no fewer than 134 wedge tombs, many of them on the rocky southwestern peninsulae or the higher hinterland of Cork to the east. In Ireland as a whole there are probably 400 wedge tombs. They are dated to a period of two or three

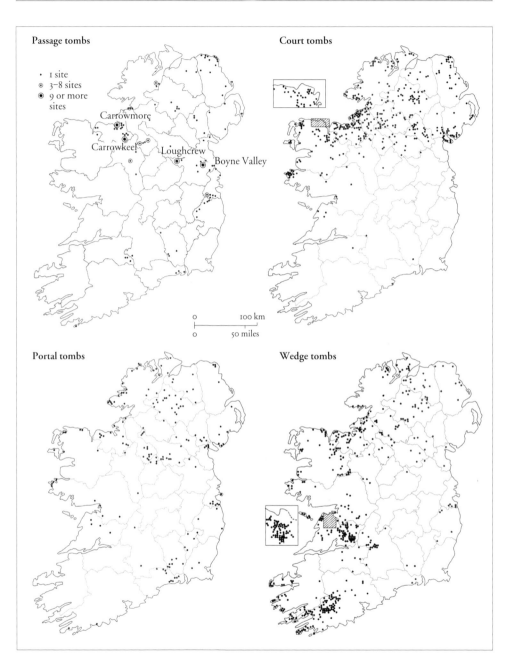

Passage tombs

· 1 site
⊙ 3–8 sites
⊙ 9 or more
  sites

Carrowmore
Carrowkeel
Loughcrew
Boyne Valley

0   100 km
0   50 miles

Court tombs

Portal tombs

Wedge tombs

centuries between 2400 and 2100 BC. This makes them contemporary with the Clava cairns of eastern Scotland and with the later stages in the Stonehenge sequence. Yet wedge tombs raise an important question. How far should they be considered a direct continuation of the earlier Irish tomb-building tradition, given that they are separated in

Distribution of the four principal categories of megalithic tomb in Ireland.

Reconstruction of the wedge tomb at Island, Co. Cork.

time from the latest passage, court and portal graves by at least 500 years? Was there indeed a single megalithic tradition in Ireland during the Neolithic, or a number of separate episodes of tomb construction, some of them drawing inspiration from earlier monuments which were up to 1000 years old?

Wedge tombs range from simple box-like forms constructed of large stone slabs to longer galleries, sometimes with a chamber at the end. All of them, however, are distinguished by decreasing height away from the entrance; hence the term 'wedge' tomb. Wedge tombs generally contained cremated remains, and opened towards the west or southwest and thus faced the sea and the setting sun. This sunset orientation marks a departure from the earlier passage tomb tradition where entrances faced towards the east, and, most famously at Newgrange, towards the winter solstice. We can be sure, furthermore, that the sunrise orientation of Newgrange was not simply a regional tradition restricted to eastern Ireland. The Clear Island passage tomb of County Cork, a southwestern outlier of the main Irish passage tomb distribution, incorporated a summer solstice sunrise orientation. Wedge tombs, by contrast, face the setting sun and the western horizon. These directions may have been specially associated with death. The absence of a passage meant that the interior of the chamber would have been directly lit by the setting sun, a fact that once again emphasizes the likely significance of the sunset orientation. In one sense, wedge tombs indicate continuity with earlier traditions: in the use of cremation and in their interest in the sun. On the other hand, the switch from a focus on sunrise to sunset reveals a significant change in beliefs since the passage tomb era some 1000 years before.

Still later in date than the wedge tombs are the so-called 'boulder burials' of Cork and Kerry. These consist typically of three or four small uprights on which a large boulder has been placed as a capstone. The space beneath is not tall enough to form a chamber and there are no chamber side walls, nor evidence of a covering mound or cairn. These really then are grave markers rather than chamber tombs – if indeed we can be certain that they had a funerary significance at all, though some boulder burials, at least, cover pits containing fragments of charcoal and cremated bone. About 80 boulder burials are known, mainly as single monuments though occasionally they are found in groups and they are sometimes inside or adjacent to stone circles. They probably belong to the later Bronze Age (1500–800 BC). Hence despite the simplicity of their form, they do not represent an early formative phase of Irish megalithic architecture; they are not the Irish equivalent of the 'dolmens' or dysser of Denmark and northern Europe.

Stone settings and earthen rings

There are over 100 small stone circles in counties Cork and Kerry, the heartland of the wedge tombs and boulder burials. Like the latter, the circles appear to date to the Middle or Late Bronze Age. One of the most famous is Drombeg in Cork, which measures a little over 9 m (30 ft) in diameter and has an entrance flanked by taller portal stones to the northeast and a recumbent stone (laid horizontally) at the southwest. Portal and recumbent stone form an axis of view which aligns with a notch in the hillside behind, where the sun sets at the

Drombeg stone circle, Co. Cork.

winter solstice. This is one of the best examples of solar alignment at these stone circles and provides a further link with the wedge tombs. Though the wedge tombs were no longer being built at this period they were still receiving secondary offerings, sometimes in pits dug within the chamber.

In this same region of southwest Ireland, there is a concentration of short stone rows comprising between three and six standing stones – over 80 sites in total, plus around 100 pairs of standing stones. The recurrent orientation is once again from northwest to southwest, and is sometimes emphasized by the carefully graduated height of the individual stones. These monuments confirm that in this part of Ireland during the later Bronze Age, the direction of sunset held a special significance.

Compared with the very numerous stone rows of southwest Ireland, northern Ireland has rather fewer monuments of this kind. It does, however, have one of the most remarkable complexes of standing stones, a site comparable in its complexity with the better-known Callanish in the Hebrides. This is Beaghmore in County Tyrone, where three pairs of stone circles are associated with a seventh 'distorted' stone circle and a number of stone rows and cairns. The stones

Stone circles and avenues at Beaghmore, Co. Tyrone.

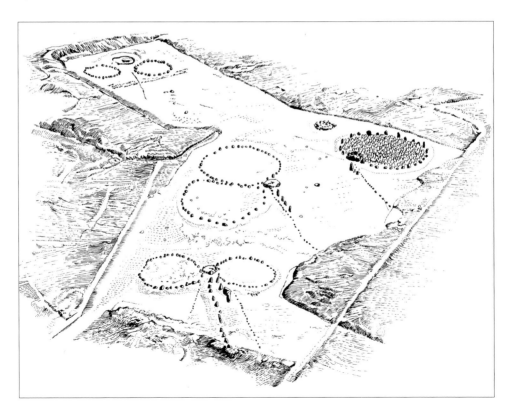

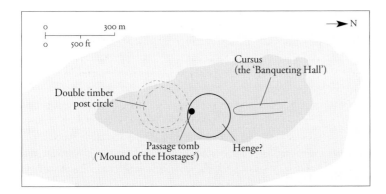

are modest in size (scarcely 'megalithic') and the circles small in scale compared with the massive rings of Orkney, Cumbria or Wessex. The largest of the Beaghmore circles (C and D) measure a mere 16–17 m (52–56 ft) across. Parallel lines of stones run northwestwards from these circles: one from between circles G and F at the southern end of the complex; one each from circles C and D and from the 'distorted' circle E; another four (spreading out fan-wise) from between circles A and B. These rows cross the collapsed remains of dry-stone field walls, further testimony of Neolithic land division in Ireland. The Beagh-more rows and circles themselves date to the 2nd millennium BC, if the dates from the cairns are to be believed. Some of the cairns con-tained human remains; some of them enclosed small slab-built cists. In one of them was found a polished stone axe of porcellanite, from the Neolithic axe quarries at Tievebulliagh and Rathlin Island, and there was other evidence of Neolithic activity (in the form of pits, pots and flints) at the site, hinting, perhaps, at a Neolithic origin for this essentially Bronze Age complex.

While most of the stone circles of Ireland appear to date to the Bronze Age rather than the Neolithic, this is not entirely the case. At Ballynoe on the northeast coast, or inland further south in the Wicklow mountains, are stone circles that bear close comparison with those of Cumbria and may testify to contacts across the Irish Sea. They could be the complement to the megalithic art found at Bryn Celli Ddu and Barclodiad y Gawres in North Wales. Ireland also has a growing number of recorded earthwork monuments, including henges and cursus monuments, analogous to those of Britain. At Fourknocks, 30 km (18 miles) north of Dublin, a pair of Neolithic chamber tombs overlooks a group of three henges and a further mound located on lower ground. At Ballynahatty in County Down, a passage tomb sits near the centre of a large earthwork henge 190 m (623 ft) across, the largest such monument in Ireland. To the north of this was a double ring of timber posts, discovered by aerial photogra-phy, and a useful reminder that timber as well as earth and stone were deployed to create these monumental sites. The important site of Tara northwest of Dublin, famous in the early Middle Ages as the seat of the High Kings of Ireland, presents a further complex of Neolithic monuments: a concentric double circle of timber posts, followed by a small passage tomb – the so-called 'Mound of the Hostages' – that was itself subsequently enclosed within an earthwork henge. A further earthwork monument, a cursus known traditionally as the 'Banqueting Hall', begins a short distance from the northern edge of the henge.

Tara, Ballynahatty and Fourknocks exemplify two important features that Irish Neolithic monuments share with their British counterparts. The first is their tendency to cluster together. An initial monument, be it tomb, henge or circle, provided a focus of ritual importance which attracted the construction of further monuments in its immediate vicinity. The passage tomb cemeteries of Loughcrew, Carrowmore and Carrowkeel illustrate the same tendency in slightly different form. The second important feature is the combination at many of these sites of monuments of different construction, incorporating timber, earth and stone. The most famous of all such Irish monument complexes is without question that which developed around Knowth, Dowth and Newgrange in the Boyne valley. As we have seen, here at Brú na Bóinne monuments of timber, earth and stone are found in close proximity. Such monument clusters must have been places of outstanding significance to the Neolithic communities of Ireland just as were Avebury, Stonehenge or the Stenness and Brodgar area of Orkney within their respective regions.

The fact that the Neolithic populations of Britain and Ireland were probably quite small makes these monument complexes all the more significant. They seem generally to have involved mortuary activity (or at least human remains), but in a context perhaps of feasting and ritual that extended beyond the purely funerary domain. Their very prominence tells us something about an attitude to landscape, to marking out or indeed to making places of special significance, that only began with the Neolithic. The adoption of pottery and domesticates did not just involve a change of diet or subsistence, but a new way of thinking about the world.

CHAPTER SIX

Neolithic monuments in their
European setting

THE NEOLITHIC MONUMENTS OF BRITAIN AND IRELAND ARE PART OF the broader family of megalithic and non-megalithic monuments distributed throughout western and northern Europe, from Iberia to Scandinavia. Earlier writers were impressed by the similarity between the monuments of these different areas and sought to interpret them in terms of a spread of megaliths (and possibly megalithic missionaries) from the Mediterranean to northern Europe along the Atlantic seaboard. As radiocarbon dates multiplied in the 1960s and 1970s, the chronology of the monuments became clearer, and a pattern emerged which suggested that megalithic monuments could have developed in parallel in several regions, notably Portugal, Brittany and Ireland. From this it was a short step to proposing a model of independent origins for the megalithic monuments of these regions. Thus an earlier theory of diffusion along the Atlantic façade of Europe gave way to a theory of multiple independent origins.

The multiregional explanation has been weakened since the 1980s by a careful reassessment which has cast doubt on many of the 'early' radiocarbon dates for megalithic monuments. The 5th millennium dates for Carrowmore in Ireland, for example, are now widely regarded with suspicion. Current evidence suggests that chambered tombs and associated monuments were built in France and Iberia from the middle of the 5th millennium and in Britain, Ireland and northern Europe from the early 4th millennium BC. Along with revisions to the chronology there has been growing acceptance that while monument traditions must be studied and understood within their local and regional contexts, adjacent parts of Atlantic Europe did not develop completely in isolation from each other. Interregional contacts can sometimes be demonstrated by flows of raw material. Northern Ireland, for example, was connected to southwest Scotland by the traffic in polished stone axes. Some 180 axes of porcellanite from Tievebulliagh and Rathlin Island in northern Ireland have been found in Britain. These are balanced by approximately 100 axes of Great Langdale tuff (from northwest England) that travelled to Ireland. Connections across the Channel or the North Sea are demonstrated by the quantity of polished stone axes of Alpine jadeite (almost 100) found in Britain, and the dolerite axes from Brittany (though only a handful) that have come to light in southwest England.

How do the Neolithic monuments fit into this background? On the one hand, several British and Irish monument types have no analogies in other parts of Atlantic Europe. Henges and cursus monuments are not found outside Britain and Ireland. Stone circles are less common elsewhere, and those of Brittany, for example, are often hemicycles or horseshoes rather than complete rings. Rows and avenues of standing stones, on the other hand, are well represented in Brittany, but this does not necessarily indicate a close connection between the monuments of the two areas. There is nothing strictly comparable to the Carnac stone rows in Britain or Ireland, especially since the multiple stone rows and fan-shaped arrangements of northern Scotland appear to date to the Bronze Age. They are all part of a generalized and widespread Atlantic tradition of standing stones that extends into later periods.

Burial mounds and chambered tombs suggest more specific inter-regional comparisons. Unchambered long mounds, for example, are a feature not only of southern and eastern Britain but are closely paralleled in south Scandinavia. Monuments such as Bygholm Norremark in Denmark illustrate the same kind of sequence – from timber mortuary structures to unchambered long mound to megalithic chambered mound – that has been documented at sites such as Wayland's Smithy in southern England. Unchambered long mounds are also found in northern and western France. The site of Le Cruchaud in Charente-Maritime with its chalk fill and turf-stack construction is strikingly reminiscent of south British long mounds such as Thickthorn Down in Dorset.

The passage graves of Britain and Ireland have analogues at a general level throughout Atlantic Europe. It may be that this specific architectural model spread widely among interlinked communities. Or the key development may have been a set of particular mortuary practices that required repeated access to the burial chamber (for the addition of new bodies or the removal or sorting of bones). Close parallels between the transepted chambers of the Cotswold-Severn tombs and the transepted chamber tombs of the Loire estuary, on the other hand, could simply be fortuitous, and it is perhaps more convincing to regard each of these regional types as the product of local development from earlier tomb forms. That said, the movement of people and ideas should not be discounted. While we may be cautious about a specific link between southwest Britain and southern Brit-

The long mound of Thickthorn Down, showing the turf structures discovered in the excavations of Drew & Piggott (1933).

tany, contact across the Irish Sea is much easier to envisage, and the portal dolmens of southwest Britain may indeed share a common origin with the portal tombs of Ireland.

Probably the clearest evidence of maritime contacts among the builders of megalithic tombs is provided by megalithic art. The Brú na Bóinne complex in Ireland has the largest concentration of megalithic art in western Europe. Knowth alone has more than 300 decorated slabs. On the opposite side of the Irish Sea in Britain, however, comparable art has hitherto been found only in two areas: in North Wales and Orkney. It may be significant also that both the North Wales sites were passage graves: Bryn Celli Ddu and Barclodiad y Gawres (though in the former the megalithic art was restricted to a single slab that was reincorporated from a pre-passage grave phase). A third decorated site at Calderstones near Liverpool was probably also

Internal turf structures in the long mound of Le Cruchaud at Sainte-Lheurine (Charente-Maritime) exposed by the excavations of Claude Burnez and Catherine Louboutin.

*Decorated kerbstone
no. 74 of the central
cairn at Knowth.*

a passage grave. Are the passage graves as well as the megalithic art tes-timony to connections across the Irish Sea?

In Orkney, few sites with 'classic' megalithic art are known: Holm of Papa Westray, Eday Manse and Pickaquoy, plus the remarkable decorated slab from Pierowall Quarry. These too may be evidence of connections with Ireland via maritime routes up the west coast of Scotland. The recent discoveries of thin incised lines at several Orkney sites that were referred to earlier, however, suggest that Orkney tombs once had painted decoration that no longer survives. The lost art that once decorated megalithic tombs, or indeed standing stones in the open air, may have revealed a variety of stylistic tradi-tions, some local, some perhaps interregional in their distribution.

Looking still further afield, the megalithic art of Britain and Ireland is part of a more widespread phenomenon that extends to northern France and Iberia. Here again there are regionally specific styles as well as motifs that recur across widely separated regions. There are also carvings on open-air rock surfaces (rock art) of the same period, and these rock art motifs overlap with those found in megalithic tombs. They serve once again to suggest a network of con-nections or common understandings that linked communities together. Whether the craftsmen who decorated the Boyne tombs had seen the megalithic art of Gavrinis (or vice versa) must remain both speculative and controversial. What should be underlined is that the Neolithic communities of Britain and Ireland were inventive, but not entirely isolated. In creating their monuments, they drew most heavily perhaps on local traditions, on the visible product of previous generations, with its specific beliefs and associations. Yet they were also linked into a wider world.

Bibliography

Armit, I., Murphy. E., Nelis, E. & Simpson, D. (eds), 2003. *Neolithic Settlement in Ireland and Western Britain.* Oxford: Oxbow Books.

Ashbee, P., 1966. 'The Fussell's Lodge Long Barrow Excavations 1957'. *Archaeologia* 100, 1–80.

Ashbee, P., Smith, I. F. & Evans, J. G., 1979. 'Excavation of three long barrows near Avebury, Wiltshire'. *Proceedings of the Prehistoric Society* 45, 207–300.

Ashmore, P., 1996. *Neolithic and Bronze Age Scotland.* London: Batsford/Historic Scotland.

Barclay, A. & Harding, J. (eds), 1999. *Pathways and Ceremonies: the cursus monuments of Britain and Ireland.* Oxford: Oxbow Books.

Barclay, G. J. & Maxwell, G. S., 1998. *The Cleaven Dyke and Littleour: monuments in the Neolithic of Tayside.* Edinburgh: Society of Antiquaries of Scotland.

Bergh, S., 1995. *Landscape of the Monuments: a study of the passage tombs in the Cúil Irra region.* Stockholm : Riksantikvarieämbetet.

Bradley, R., 1998. *The Significance of Monuments.* London: Routledge.

Bradley, R., 2000. *The Good Stones : a new investigation of the Clava cairns.* Edinburgh : Society of Antiquaries of Scotland.

Bradley, R., 2005. *The Moon and the Bonfire. An Investigation of Three Stone Circles in North-east Scotland.* Edinburgh: Society of Antiquaries of Scotland.

Burl, A., 2000. *The Stone Circles of Britain, Ireland and Brittany.* New Haven & London: Yale University Press.

Chippindale, C., 2004. *Stonehenge Complete* (new edition). London & New York: Thames & Hudson.

Cleal, R. M. J., Walker, K. E. & Montague, R., 1995. *Stonehenge in its Landscape: twentieth-century excavations.* London: English Heritage.

Coles, B. J. 1998. 'Doggerland: a speculative survey'. *Proceedings of the Prehistoric Society* 64, 45–81.

Cooney, G., 2000. *Landscapes of Neolithic Ireland.* London: Routledge.

Cummings, V. & Fowler, C. (eds), 2004. *The Neolithic of the Irish Sea: materiality and traditions of practice.* Oxford: Oxbow Books.

Cummings, V. & Pannett, A. (eds.), 2005. *Set in Stone. New approaches to Neolithic monuments in Scotland.* Oxford: Oxbow Books.

Cummings, V. & Whittle, A., 2004. *Places of Special Virtue : megaliths in the Neolithic landscapes of Wales.* Oxford: Oxbow Books.

Darvill, T., 2004. *Long Barrows of the Cotswolds and surrounding areas.* Stroud: Tempus.

Edmonds, M., 1999. Ancestral Geographies of the Neolithic. Landscapes, monuments and memory. London: Routledge.

Eogan, G., 1986. Knowth and the Passage Tombs of Ireland. London: Thames & Hudson.

Fairweather, A. D. & Ralston, I. B. M., 1993. 'The Neolithic timber hall at Balbridie, Grampian Region, Scotland: the building, the date, the plant macrofossils'. *Antiquity* 67, 313–23.

Gibson, A. M., 1998. *Stonehenge & Timber Circles.* Stroud: Tempus.

Gillings, M., & Pollard, J., 2004. *Avebury.* London: Duckworth.

Harding, J., 2003. *Henge Monuments of the British Isles.* Stroud: Tempus.

Hedges, J., 1984. *Tomb of the Eagles.* London: Murray.

Lucas, G. M., 1996. 'Of death and debt. A history of the body in Neolithic and Early Bronze Age Yorkshire'. *Journal of European Archaeology* 4, 99–118.

O'Kelly, M. J., 1982. *Newgrange. Archaeology, art and legend.* London: Thames & Hudson.

Oswald, A., Dyer, C. & Barber, M., 2001. *The Creation of Monuments. Neolithic Causewayed Enclosures in the British Isles.* London: English Heritage.

Piggott, S., 1962. *The West Kennet Long Barrow. Excavations 1955–6.* London: HMSO.

Pollard, J. & Reynolds, A., 2002. *Avebury: The biography of a landscape.* Stroud: Tempus.

Richards, C., 1996. 'Monuments as landscape: creating the centre of the world in late Neolithic Orkney'. *World Archaeology* 28, 190–208.

Ritchie, A. (ed.), 2000. *Neolithic Orkney in its European Context.* Cambridge: McDonald Institute for Archaeological Research.

Ruggles, C. L. N., 1999. *Astronomy in Prehistoric*

Britain and Ireland. New Haven &London: Yale University Press.

Saville, A., 1990. *Hazleton North: the excavation of a Neolithic long cairn of the Cotswold-Severn group.* London: Historic Buildings and Monuments Commission for England.

Schulting, R. J. & Richards, M. P., 2002. 'The wet, the wild and the domesticated: the Mesolithic-Neolithic transition on the west coast of Scotland'. *European Journal of Archaeology* 5, 147–89.

Shee Twohig, E., 1981. *The Megalithic Art of Western Europe.* Oxford: Clarendon Press.

Smith, I. F., 1965. *Windmill Hill and Avebury: excavations by Alexander Keiller, 1925–1939.* Oxford: Clarendon Press.

Thomas, J., 1999. *Understanding the Neolithic.* London: Routledge.

Thomas, J. & Whittle, A., 1986. 'Anatomy of a tomb: West Kennet revisited'. *Oxford Journal of Archaeology* 5, 129–156.

Tilley, C., 1994. *A Phenomenology of Landscape. Places, paths and monuments.* Oxford: Berg.

Vyner, B. E., 1984. 'The excavation of a Neolithic cairn at Street House, Loftus, Cleveland'. *Proceedings of the Prehistoric Society* 50, 151–95.

Watson, A. & Keating, D., 1999. 'Architecture and sound: an acoustic analysis of megalithic monuments in prehistoric Britain'. *Antiquity* 73, 325–36.

Watson, A. & Keating, D., 2000. 'The architecture of sound in Neolithic Orkney', in Ritchie, A. (ed.) *Neolithic Orkney in its European Context.* Cambridge: McDonald Institute for Archaeological Research, 259–63.

Whittle, A., 1997. *Sacred Mound, Holy Rings: Silbury Hill and the West Kennet palisade enclosures : a later Neolithic complex in north Wiltshire.* Oxford : Oxbow Books.

Whittle, A., Pollard, J. & Grigson, C., 1999. *The Harmony of Symbols: the Windmill Hill causewayed enclosure, Wiltshire.* Oxford : Oxbow Books.

Acknowledgments

This book has its origins in an invitation I received a few years ago to write a short account of British and Irish megalithic monuments for a French readership. The eventual outcome was *Monuments mégalithiques de Grande-Bretagne et d'Irlande*, published by Errance in 2005. Several British colleagues observed that an English edition of the book would be very useful both for students and the general reader, and I am delighted that Thames & Hudson (with whom I have published for several years) have been keen to take this on. My thanks go to Colin Ridler and all at Thames & Hudson for their help in seeing this edition through to a successful conclusion, and to Frédéric Lontcho of Errance for his assistance with the original French edition.

Apart from the language, the text of the present English edition differs only slightly from the French edition, although I have taken the opportunity to modify and update it in a number of places. Several of the illustrations are also new to this edition.

A special debt of thanks is owed to all those colleagues who helped me in the writing of this book, and especially those who supplied photos or other illustrations, or who kindly gave me permission to reproduce them here. I am grateful also to Dora Kemp for her help with the preparation of the diagrams that appear on pp. 52, 85 & 126.

Sources of illustrations

Professor Bryony Coles and Sue Rouillard; Dr Neil Brodie; Dr Andrew Jones (p. 16); Blaze O'Connor (p. 16); Lindsay Jones & English Heritage (pp. 19, 94 & 118); Ms Eve O'Kelly (pp. 20 & 138); Liz Cooper & Oxford University Press (p. 22); Rose Desmond & Cambridge University Committee for Aerial Photography (pp. 23, 90, 99 & 103); Mr Reay Robertson Mackay & Mrs M. E. Robertson-Mackay (p. 24); Mr David Hogg & Dr Gordon Barclay (p. 26); Mr Patrick & Historic Scotland (pp. 27 & 55); Dr Kenneth Brophy (p. 26); Dr Gordon Barclay (p. 31); Dr Vicki Cummings (p. 33); the late Dr Graham Ritchie & Royal Commission on the Ancient and Historical Monuments of Scotland (pp. 34 & 42); Dr Alison Sheridan (p. 35); Dr Aubrey Burl (pp. 37 & 62); Dr Audrey Henshall (pp. 38, 45a, 46 & 56); Professor Richard Bradley (pp. 41, 58, 60 & 75); Mr Stuart Reilly (pp. 45, 50a & 51); Mr Adam Welfare & Royal Commission on the Ancient and Historical Monuments of Scotland (p. 61); Dr Elizabeth Shee Twohig (p. 75); Dr Alan Saville (p. 80); Mr Blaise Vyner (p. 82); Mr Chris Evans (p. 83); Dr Ruth Morgan (p. 84); Dr Paul Ashbee (p. 84); Dr Ian Kinnes (p. 87a); Dr Jan Harding (p. 91); Dr Robert Johnston (p. 96); Mr Andrew David & English Heritage (p. 94); Mr Tony Daly & National Museums & Galleries of Wales (p. 95); Oxford University Press (New York) (p. 119); Dr Andrew Fitzpatrick & Wessex Archaeology (pp. 124); Dr Eoin Grogan (p. 126); Dr Stefan Bergh (p. 129); Professor George Eogan (pp. 140, 141 & 154); Professor John Waddell (p. 145); Dr Catherine Louboutin (p. 153); David Pearce of the Rock Art Research Institute, University of the Witwatersrand (colour plates 5, 9, 10, 18, 19.

Colour plates

1 Chris Scarre 2 Photo Mike Pitts 3 Chris Scarre 4 Photo Mike Pitts 5 D. G. Pearce, RARI 6 Chris Scarre 7 Chris Scarre 8 Chris Scarre 9 D. G. Pearce, RARI 10 D. G. Pearce, RARI 11 Photo Mike Pitts 12 Photo Mike Pitts 13 Photo Mike Pitts 14 Photo Mike Pitts 15 Photo © Hugh Palmer 16 Michael Jenner 17 Duchas 18 D. G. Pearce, RARI 19 D. G. Pearce, RARI 20 Photo © Hugh Palmer

Text illustrations, by page number. **a** above; **c** centre; **b** below; **l** left; **r** right

Title-page Edwin Smith **6** *Archaeologia Cambrensis* 11, 1865 **9** after Bryony Coles 1998 **11** Caulfield 1998 **13** Cleal, Walker & Montague 1995 **15** Gabriel Cooney 2000 **16a** 16bl Andrew Jones 1999 **16br** Blaze O'Conno **17** Cambridge University Committee for Aerial Photography **18** Chris Scarre **19** Cleal et al. © English Heritage **20** Eve O'Kelly 1982 **21** after Aubrey Burl 1981 **22** Alexander Thom © Oxford University Press **23** Callanish **24a** Frédéric Lontcho **24b** R. & M. E. Robertson-Mackay **26al** Gordon Barclay **26ar** David Hogg **26b** Kenneth Brophy 1998 **27a** Coles & Simpson 1965 **27b** Patrick Ashmore © Historic Scotland **28** Masters 1973 **29** Piggott 1972 **30** after Mercer 1981 & Mercer et al. 1988 **31** Gordon Barclay **32** Corcoran 1969 **33a** after Hughes 1988 **33b** Vicki Cummings **34** Graham Ritchie: Crown Copyright; Royal Commission on the Ancient and Historical Monuments of Scotland **35** Sheridan 2003 **37** Aubrey Burl 1976 **38** Davidson & Henshall 1989 **39a** Frédéric Lontcho **39b** Crown Copyright; Royal Commission on the Ancient and Historical Monuments of Scotland **40** Edwin Smith **41a** Bradley et al. 2001 **41b** Chris Scarre **42** Ritchie 1976, © Historic Scotland **43a** after Richards 1996 **43b** watercolour 1865 **44** after Richards 1996 **45a, 45b** Henshall 1985 **46** Davidson & Henshall 1989 **47a** Chris Scarre **47b** Childe 1931 **48a** Chris Scarre **48b** Frédéric Lontcho **49** Chris Scarre **50a, 50b, 50c, 51** Reilly 2003 **52l** after Hedges 1984 **52r, 53** Hedges 1984 **54** after Davidson & Henshall 1989 **55** Ashmore 1996, © Historic Scotland **56a** Davidson & Henshall 1991 **56b** Chris Scarre **57** Chris Scarre **58** Richard Bradley **59a, 59b** Chris Scarre **60** Richard Bradley 2002 **61** Crown Copyright Royal Commission on the Ancient and Historical Monuments of Scotland **62** Burl 1976 **63** Frédéric Lontcho **64** after Darvill 1987 & Kinnes 1992, with additions **73** after Powell 1973 **74a, 74b** Frédéric Lontcho **75a** Shee Twohig 1981 **75b** Bradley 1998 **76** after Berry 1930 & Piggott 1962 **77a** Frédéric Lontcho **77b** Chris Scarre **79a** Frédéric Lontcho **79b** drawing Stuart Piggott; © Crown Copyright **80a, 80b** Alan Saville **81** Grimes 1939 **82** Vyner 1984 **83a** Chris Evans **83b** Evans & Hodder forthcoming **84a** Morgan 1990 **84b** Ashbee 1966 **85** after Ashbee 1966 **86** after Bradley 1992 & Barclay & Halpin 1998 **87a** Kinnes et al. 1983 **87b** Mortimer 1905 **89** Robert Johnston 1999 **90** Cambridge University Committee for Aerial Photography **91** J. Harding 2003 **93** Edwin Smith **94** Andrew David, © English Heritage **95a** after Gibson 1994 **95b** drawing Tony Daly, © Amgueddfa ac Orielau Cenedlaethol Cymru/National Galleries of Wales **96** after Whittle 1993 **98** Edwin Smith **99** Cambridge Committee for Aerial Photography **100** after Ashbee et al. 1979 **103** Cambridge University Committee for Aerial Photography **104a** British Tourist Authority **104b** H. St George Gray collection **113** Smith 1965 **114a** William Stukeley **114b** after Pollard & Reynolds 2002 **115a** after Whittle 1997 **115b** Frédéric Lontcho **117** Chris Scarre **118a** Frédéric Lontcho **118b** © English Heritage. **119a** © Oxford University Press **121** after Ruggles 1999 **122** Stuart Piggott 1940 **123** Clark 1936 **124l, 125r** Wessex Archaeology **126** after Grogan 2004 **127a** O'Nuaillain 1972 **127b** after Carleton Jones **129a** Bergh 1995 **129b** Chris Scarre **130** Chris Scarre **132a** Hencken 1939 **132b** Frédéric Lontcho **133** Cooney 2000 **134** Edwin Smith **136b** Frédéric Lontcho **137** O'Kelly 1982 **138** O'Kelly 1982 **139a, 139b** Chris Scarre **140a, 140b** George Eogan **141a**, George Eogan **141c** after Eogan 1986 **141b** Duchas **143** D. L. Swan **145** Waddell 1998 **146** after Fahy & O'Kelly 1958 **147** © Commissioners of Public Works in Ireland **148** Harbison 1988 **149** after Cooney 2000 **153b** Claude Burnez/Catherine Louboutin **154** George Eogan

Index